The Only Online Marketing Book You Need for Your Small Business

Includes 8 Actionable Steps to Amazing Online Marketing

Warren Laine-Naida & Bridget Willard

Dedication

My thanks go to the countless small business and entrepreneur clients I have had the chance to work with and learn from since creating my first website in 1994. Without you, this book would not have been possible. - Warren

This book is dedicated to small business owners rolling up their sleeves to make their dreams work. I always say, "there is no dream without the work," and you're doing it. You know you need to market your business, and I know you have limited time. Learn to do it the right way, efficiently, and your bottom line will see the difference. - Bridget

Introduction

What do we mean by "Small Business?" We're all small businesses. We market and sell ourselves each and every day in how we dress, what brands we choose, where we eat and shop, how we act on social media, what movies we watch, or which car we drive.

A small business can be a one-person business or a group of people working together in a store or an office. Depending on your industry, a small business can have as many as 250 employees! Small can be big – it's all a question of perspective.

Warren has been working since the middle 1970's – like many of us -- with a paper route and a stint at McDonald's. The world has changed a lot since then. Now we can shop, find information, communicate, and be entertained at home using our mobile phone. He has been working in marketing and sales in Canada since the 1980s, starting in online marketing and web development after moving to Germany in 1994.

Bridget has been working since she was fourteen doing accounting for a pizza shop, office work at a publisher, a large military school, a trucking company, a church, and transitioned to office and accounting in the construction field. In 2009, she began her marketing career at an advertising agency and became a freelance consultant in 2017. The variety of clients we've both worked with is to your benefit.

In our lifetimes, pen and paper have been replaced by the fax machine in our kitchen, replaced by a smart refrigerator and Alexa ordering our shopping.

In his current role as a digital consultant, Warren has worked on over 350 digital projects for more than 150 clients in 12 countries. That experience is channeled into teaching adults, children, and seniors how to use the tools and skills necessary in our digital world. Second, he advises and assists small businesses, nonprofits, schools, and organizations. Why? As the internet and internet-connected devices become integral to our lives, it becomes necessary that everyone learns how to use them. Having a digital competency is essential if we want to ensure our participation in a democratic society.

In her current role as CEO and marketing consultant, Bridget writes copy for several clients and manages about a dozen social media accounts, plus or minus five. She's worked heavily with nonprofits, both as a staff member and a vendor. She's been involved in the franchise development industry. She now specializes in business-to-business marketing for WordPress products and services and is one of the best in her niche.

This book is intended to help you begin or improve upon online marketing for your small business. We also hope to fuel your interest and excitement about what digital offers us. Your digital presence is an extension of all the things your business does online and offline. It's an exciting time!

Online marketing and communication is a way for you to make new connections and share with the world. It's a foundational skill that you can apply to grow your business for years to come, no matter how quickly technology changes and trends rise and fall.

If you're not as tech literate as you'd like to be, that's okay. Communication, online or offline, is not a contest. Participate. Try. Fail. Learn. Try again. Succeed!

Warren Laine-Naida
Bremen, Germany
WarrenLaineNaida.net

Bridget Willard
San Antonio, USA
BridgetWillard.com

March 2021

Online Marketing in 8 Steps

Increase Your Knowledge

Your Website - Your Online Marketing Hub

Your website may be the first impression your customer has of your business. It is available around the world, twenty-four hours a day, seven days a week. Even on holidays! It may be your audience's only experience with you.

Your website offers you so many advantages over traditional and more expensive media:

- It is (should be) always up-to-date
- Offers customer support and information when you're closed
- Offers an online shop when you're closed
- It is individual and unique to you
- Increases your visibility around the entire world

With all of these advantages at the click of a mouse, having a website is essential. With the many tools now available to you, it's easier to create and maintain than ever.

Please read more about building a website in the "Build That Website!" Section (Step 2).

Step 1 -- An Introduction to Online Marketing

What is Marketing? The American Marketing Association[1] defines marketing as being " … the activity, set of institutions, and processes for creating, communicating, delivering, and exchanging offerings that have value for customers, clients, partners, and society at large."

Marketing is not a new activity. Wine urns found in the ruins of Pompei from 70 AD were marked with flavourful descriptions of the wine they once contained. Classified ads ran in newspapers in Germany in the 1600s. Benjamin Franklin founded his Poor Richard's Almanac in the 1700s to market his printing business - one of the earliest Content Marketing examples.

The Consumer Culture we know today began in the early 1900s with the invention of cinema, radio, television, and the telephone. Our digital age started as early as the 1970s with ARPANET and the first messages sent between Stanford and MIT, opening the world of fax, email, internet, and mobile and app marketing.

What will tomorrow bring? Virtual and augmented reality marketing is already reaching out their fingers and meeting with

---

[1] https://www.ama.org/the-definition-of-marketing-what-is-marketing

Alexa and Siri's voices in the first generation of what is sure to be an incredible new world of marketing.

A lot may sound like a foreign language, especially if you're new to online marketing, but the skills you learn here will help your business stand out, grow, and reach more customers than ever. Assisting small business entrepreneurs to grow and reach their goals is what drives us. So, buckle up, small business owner - and welcome to the future!

Explain Marketing to a Five-Year-Old

If your picture is cool, people will notice it within 3 seconds. If they like it, they will look at it for 30 seconds. If they love it, they will talk about it for 300 seconds.

Marketing Never Sleeps

Are you trying to figure out the best way to communicate with prospective customers? Do you use email or social media? Do you prefer telephone contact, messaging, or a written letter? What's the best way for you to meet customer's needs in a fast-changing & highly competitive online environment?

Today we are almost always connected to our phones. Studies suggest 90% of us wake up and go to sleep with our smartphones. That level of distraction is a double-edged sword; people have access to information at the touch of a finger, and we are targeted by advertising 24/7. We need to be savvy enough to match the customer journey and the many new ways our people collect and use our marketing and communication tools and techniques.

The Customer Journey

David Ogilvy once said, "The customer is not a moron – they are your wife." (Ogilvy[2]) In the same spirit, the customer journey is not some mythical quest. We all take customer journeys – multiple journeys – every day – and sometimes we sit on two trains going in different directions simultaneously.

---

[2] Confessions of an Advertising Man David Ogilvy Atheneum Books 1963

What is The Customer Journey? This is the path we take when deciding we want something to the point after purchasing an item.

The Customer Journey does not stop and start – it's always happening. It's like wanting a coffee or a doughnut – people want something – but we shop differently, so our journeys are unique. We don't buy a car on a whim at the check-out counter. On the other hand, some people plan their coffee purchases as part of their commute every day. They don't think about it at all. After a sale, before a sale, it's all a part of the Customer Journey in between sales.

Companies have long understood their customer's journey and how to use different tactics to move them towards a purchase. Mobile has changed that – now that we can shop anytime and anywhere, it's more about Micro-Moments[3] than a planned journey.

At the heart of it all is one simple thing – need. Satisfying a need. Solving a problem. If you understand that, you understand the Customer Journey. You understand people's intent.

---

[3] https://www.thinkwithgoogle.com/marketing-strategies/micro-moments/

What is a Customer?

eCommerce and the Mobile Internet are redefining the Customer Journey, specifically our interactions with each other, but wait, who are our Customers, our Users, or Visitors even?

Customers are either Existing or Potential. They could be Employees (of our company) or multiplicators (influencers, family, friends – someone we trust or wish to emulate).

We want one of four things:

1. we want to buy something,
2. we want information,
3. we want to be entertained,
4. or we want to communicate – be a part of a community.

And we want - at all times - to be satisfied. However, times are changing. What we used to *expect* in the way of Customer Satisfaction is morphing into a *demand*. And that demand is called Customer Delight.

We have all heard of the Marketing Funnel. It is our journey through this funnel that influences and is influenced by our Intent. Traditionally we saw the Marketing Funnel as a linear process:

1. We saw an ad for or felt the need for a product.
2. Then we thought about buying a specific product.
3. And then we purchased the product.
4. Finally, we shared our experiences with others.

Thanks to our mobile phones, the Marketing Funnel has become a series of Marketing Cycles – interlocking cycles of consideration and comparison. Also, we don't just stop our relationship with a brand at the sale. We continue our connection with after-sales service, recommendations, and integrating ourselves into our customers' life journey.

With a phone in our hands, we are continually informing, judging, buying, returning, sharing, caring, hating products and brands. We have become, in many cases, our brands!

O.K. So, Where is This Heading?

We already said that eCommerce and the Mobile Internet are redefining the Customer Journey and our interactions with each other. We only need to remember a few years back when we would hear of a restaurant from a friend and maybe go based on their experiences. Now we can make that decision based on the Instagram feed of a Korean influencer we might happen to follow.

Digital is also redefining our customer experiences, the value chain, fulfillment processes, marketing, sales, and customer loyalty. As we become more catered to and become more demanding, what we used to expect in Customer Satisfaction is morphing into a demand for Customer Delight.

The Customer Journey is affected by countless micro-moments – which makes marketing very tricky. What are Micro-Moments, what influences them — how do we identify them? While a Customer Journey is the sum of experiences that customers go through, micro-moments are touchpoints at which customers act on a need.

The SEO of your website, Social Media, mainstream media, advertising online and offline, and actual contact with people, labels, smells, tastes, jingles, etc., at bricks and mortar stores, on the train, the bus … the touchpoints are ubiquitous.

Cross-device (marketing over multiple devices) and Cross-media Marketing (marketing using multiple media types) help us to be at the right place at the right time in any Customer Journey — without ruining it with too many ads, at the wrong time, or in the wrong place.

Successfully understanding the Customer Journey means understanding the right mix of your Paid, Shared, Owned, and Earned media. It means understanding how to leverage our customers and users so that they become ambassadors of your brand or product.

The Marketing Cycle means focusing on serving your customers' and users' needs in such a way today so that they trust you enough to help them tomorrow. Digital allows us to do this in an easy and manageable way, giving us more time for the important things — customer loyalty and increased customer lifetime.

Let's Talk About User Experience

User Experience. You've heard the term, and like most of us, accept it to mean how you feel using a website or accessing an app on your phone. UX defines our perceptions of aspects of a system, such as utility, ease of use, and efficiency. In marketing and sales, it is generally accepted that user experience "defines a brand."

A good user experience can involve the simple act of finding up-to-date and correct information on a website. It isn't sexy, but it can make a big difference. For our websites and those of our clients, it's good to be a stickler. Information on a website must be up-to-date. We all know how disappointed we feel reading in the paper about a sale at the Wine Shop, only to discover that we are reading last week's newspaper.

A colleague of ours registered for an advertised event (on the school website) advertised as "fragrance-free." As they suffer from MCS (Multiple Chemical Sensitivity), this was an essential piece of information. However, after arriving, they discovered many people in attendance wearing perfume. The event organizers explained that it was not mandatory while they encouraged people not to wear cologne. Try that attitude when selling "nut-free" or "meat-free" snacks and see where it lands you.

Imagine you went to a restaurant advertising lactose-free cheese, and you order it – because you are lactose intolerant.

Then it transpires that they mix the cheese half-half with regular cheese. Or imagine driving to the next town because a restaurant advertises lobster on their menu, but when you arrive, it turns out the online menu was from last week. I've been there. Have you?

Correct information on a website is not a nice to have – it is a must-have.

A good or bad User experience is not just limited to our websites.

"Technology, digital, the web should be inclusive." First, access to information and services should be open and available to all. Second, people accessing that information should find it complete. This is basic marketing, having the correct information available to all.

A Useful Experience is a Good Experience

Have you ever found items on a website that turned out to be wrong? How was your user experience then? Some of the things we've all discovered – after the fact – that were wrong on some websites:

- Opening hours – store already closed upon arrival
- Telephone number – not in service
- Prices of items – were higher in the store
- Menu items – last week's menu listed on the website
- Information is offered in another language – but the text is either a bad translation or utterly different information
- The address of your shop should be correct – the store had moved!

Up-to-date and correct information is essential to have on your website because people are accessing it, very often on their phones, locally and immediately. Possibly they are making decisions about whether to go to your restaurant or store – or book your event. If your opening hours are incorrect, or you have moved recently – well, this isn't the best user experience a potential customer can have. And they will probably tell people about it.

Users rely on your website as an accurate source of information. Sometimes it can be an inconvenience that your website is out of date – sometimes, it can be extremely costly or painful for the user. Correct information on a website is not a nice to have – it is a must-have.

Guaranteeing a good user experience is finding the sweet spot that conjures a user's physical, emotional, and cognitive needs. People will leave your store or website if they don't find what they want is as relevant to the internet as it is to a shopping mall. The difference is that we have become accustomed to finding what we want on the www quickly and moving on to other websites if we do not. A shopping mall has you, at least physically, at a more significant disadvantage.

Someone using the latest smartphone, with the fastest connection, looking at the best website ever designed, will probably have a terrible user experience if they cannot find the information they are seeking.

Content Marketing

Content Marketing is one of the many digital buzzwords you cannot avoid these days. Digital Transformation, Native Advertising, Internet of Things, Big Data, Machine Learning, Algorithm,

Customer Journey, Digital First, eHealth, Micro-Moments, and Geo-Fencing are just a few of many.

While the term Content Marketing first appeared in 1996, the idea has been with us since at least 1732 when Benjamin Franklin published his Poor Richard's Almanack to promote his own printing business.

You might be unaware of the amount of Content Marketing you see every day or how far back the practice goes. Johnson & Johnson began sending wound treatment guides to doctors as early as 1888. In 1895, John Deere published the first issue of "The Furrow," an agricultural magazine that published print advertisements. "The Michelin Guide" (Michelin Tires) began in 1900 as a free guide offering car drivers information on accommodations and auto maintenance.

We still have a free cooking book printed for young couples from 1964 and published by the Rogers Sugar Company – in addition to the many bakery items is an introduction about the importance of sugar for a healthy and growing family.

Companies have long understood how to use different tactics to move people towards a purchase. In the past, Content Marketing was practiced in print, then radio, then television, and today via websites and our smartphones. Today we talk about User Stories, User Paths, Target Group Analysis – more buzzwords, perhaps. Still, with your users multitasking across multiple devices, they are more important than ever to understand.

What is Content Marketing?

"Content Marketing is a marketing technique of creating and distributing relevant and valuable content to attract, acquire, and engage a clearly defined and understood target audience— to drive profitable customer action." (Content Marketing Institute)

Do you have a blog? That's content marketing. Do you offer a newsletter with tips and tricks? That's content marketing. Do you give away free samples? That's content marketing.

Content Marketing uses various resources (newspaper, TV show, video, blog, social media, etc.) to do three things:

- create interest in a product and/or service,
- increase sales,
- increase brand identity and trust.

Content must not also be informative for existing customers but should also speak to potential customers. Most importantly, it should add value to the product itself.

A World of Warcraft Cookbook? A great example of advertising a product with content while adding extra value.

Getting Started

Before you start your Content Marketing strategy, it is essential that you first research and understand who your target group is.

Your target group is then divided into unique segments. Content can then be created for each of these segments.

How do you know where to publish content? First, look at all channels and platforms your target group visits. Then, decide which content is best suited for each platform. What works well on Twitter is perhaps not ideal for Facebook. What works well in an in-flight magazine might not work well on your blog.

The most crucial requirement for Content Marketing is that the content speaks to your audience. People are savvy and informed consumers. For each piece of content we receive, we research three pieces on our own. We need to understand why we are writing the content, placing the images, and linking it to related information if we want it to be relevant. We need to understand the requirements of our audience.

We are Slaves to Purpose

Everything we do, every project, every hour spent on the couch or at the gym, invariably has a purpose. Without purpose, we have nothing. What is the purpose of content, and how can we manage what we are doing with it efficiently and effectively?

Your content should answer the why and how that is your (or your company's) purpose.* Ask yourself: Is my content relevant to my purpose? Will people who see my content on my website find the likely answers to their questions? Will I speak to them?

When we talk about content, two terms that are often used interchangeably are important:

- Content Strategy (Why you are creating content, who you are serving, and how you will help them in a way no one else can.), and;

- Content Plan (How you will execute your strategy, who on your team will be handling, and details like the key topics you will cover, what content you will create, when and how you will share your content, and specific calls to action you include).

Implementing the strategy and the plan is probably you, the Content Manager, or Content Marketer. Quite possibly, you, without the title, may update your site and put together a Facebook ad.

- How do you connect content with related content (user paths and stories)?

- How do you share content in a social media or marketing environment (fitting the right message to the right medium)?

- How do you write relevant and useful content that will drive people to your site? (understanding context).**

Give it to Me Straight

Three factors are essential if you are going to be successful in your content marketing.

You must be able to answer your target group's questions and needs, offer them added value within the content on your website and social media and generate interest in your other products and services.

How do you know where to put the right information for the right user? Remember, there are four things people are looking for on the web:

- Information
- Product
- Entertainment
- Conversation (Community)

Providing information to multiple users on multiple platforms is easier and cheaper today than a generation ago. It may be tempting to place the same content on all your platforms or to put too much content out there. Don't do it. With more and more companies creating more and more content on more channels, the temptation is better avoided. The most efficient way isn't always the most effective way.

Look where your customers are, direct content to that platform, and provide them with added value solutions to their needs. It's that simple.

What Were Those Asterix's I Saw?

*Brand Affinity

We buy most products because we identify with the brand. We follow and share information about brands, influencers, celebrities, etc., because we feel an affinity.

We probably buy Starbucks coffee because we identify ourselves with their brand as part of their tribe. Their politics, interior design, logo, music, and customers all go into a brand mix that is ultimately sold. Not coffee.

The same can be said about everything, from running shoes to breakfast cereal. Something about the brand touches us. By purchasing it, we are saying, "This is who I am."

More than anything else, people want to know what others are doing with your product. These indirect connections are called Brand Obsessions. It's all about speaking with your audience. "We know how you live and what you want. We get you."

**Content Strategy/User Context

A proper analysis of a user's context requires not only an understanding of users' goals, but also of their behaviors: what are they doing (carrying groceries? driving? in a meeting?), how are they feeling (lousy day? great day? fired? in love?), and what are they capable of at the time (mobile? one hand? two?)

– and that is over and above if their internet connection is working well or not …

Whether people see our content and respond is as much a matter of our understanding of their goals as it is understanding their behavior and, as much as possible, matching our content.

Next Steps -- Content Marketing Assignments

- Get out a paper and pen (or Google Docs) and write down the top ten questions customers ask you.

- What do you wish people knew about your industry?

- What other businesses pair well with your services and products?

- Do you prefer to write or shoot quick videos?

- Who is your ideal customer? Not the ones you get. The ones you want.

- We'll call your ideal customer Janet. Write 300 words to Janet on why she should choose your business.

- You just produced content. Where will you publish it

Create Your First Marketing Campaign

What do we market our product? To whom? Why? Where? How? When? It's a big job planning a marketing campaign. Here's some help!

1. Define your Goals
2. Target Group values and positioning
3. Market and competition analysis
4. Channel strategy, Measures
5. Implementation
6. Controlling and analysis
7. Optimization

Step 1. Define Your Goals

What do you want to achieve with your online marketing campaign? In other words, what do you want people to do? Marketing is about human behavior. Answering this question is the only way to measure your success later effectively. Marketers like to throw around acronyms like KPI (Key Performance Indicators) but what matters is SMART.

Specific. Measurable. Achievable. Realistic. Timely.

Specific goals lend themselves to being measurable. If you can measure it, you can probably achieve it, which, by the way, makes it real. Timely just means that you have a start date and an end date. So, you can "believe you can fly" and "touch the sky," but that isn't realistic. Instead, we've brought together a few examples of goals and their matching KPI. (See? Now you're SMART, too.)

Goals and KPI by Category

- Customer acquisition -- KPIs: number of visitors, number of new users

- Customer loyalty -- (KPI: returning users

- Brand awareness -- KPIs: social shares, reach, interactions, engagement rate

- Sales increase -- KPI: conversion rate

Your goals need to be SMART! Not, "I want more customers."

Example:

- First-quarter goal is to increase brand awareness by 10% via social media. This is specific (impressions), measurable (by 10%), realistic (not by 100%), achievable (you can tweet or post more), and timely (due 31 Mar).

- Second-quarter goal is to generate new leads for interested customers via our website and blog.

- Third-quarter goal is to sell more products via our online shop.

- Fourth-quarter goal is to generate new customers by offering existing customers a discount for their friends.

It isn't what you sell; it's how you sell it.

Step 2. Understand Your Target Group, Values, and Position

How does your brand align with customers? Where is your position in the marketplace? Defining your target group also sets your marketing campaign's tone and - if you have multiple target groups, differentiate them. If you cannot get into the minds of your customers, how will you speak to them?

You already have the advantage of knowing a lot about your existing customers, but who are your potential customers? Who are your brand ambassadors? Who are your competitors?

Example: If you want to sell a new health product for women, you need to address the target group "working women" on a different thematic and emotional level than "stay-at-home moms," "freelancers," or "office professionals." Why? It is all about their lifestyle, income level, and mostly about the context your product fits into their lives.

Step 3. Research the Marketplace and Competition

As a small business online shop owner, you'll have many questions. Where do you begin your research? There are four main areas to think about:

- General market development
- Customer analysis
- Competitor analysis
- Analysis of your market position

General Market Development

Stay up to date by evaluating existing information about your market. Look at trade journals, research industry reports, and blogs that deal with your market, and subscribe to your competitors' newsletters!

- How much revenue is generated with my products?
- How fast is my market growing?
- What are the current and upcoming trends?
- How will my market develop over the next few years?

Customer analysis

How is your customer satisfaction? - for example, with the offer, the service, the delivery.

How is your customer demand? - for example, for additional products or services.

Customer analysis is the most crucial area of market research. Look for studies on buying behavior, customer segments for your market. Keep your eye out for specialist articles on relevant online blogs.

One of the most important ways to learn what is with customer surveys. You have frequent contact with your customers, but various topics are discussed that often get lost in everyday life. You should survey your customers regularly. Use social media, email, and in-house surveys. Numerous online tools allow you to set up a survey with well-designed forms and built-in analysis, such as Survey Monkey.

The questions you ask yourself mustn't change over a long time to see any trends. If possible, ask closed questions that can be answered with yes/no or a value for grading, then you will get a precise evaluation. The last question should ask for customers' advice, such as "Do you have any suggestions or criticism?"

The fewer questions you ask, the more participants you will get - people don't like to spend a lot of time on surveys, especially if there is no incentive. Perhaps offer a gift certificate or a percentage off for completing the survey.

Competitor Analysis

When analyzing your competition, you need first to determine your relevant competitors. It's important to know who you have as competitors, where they are active, and how.

The goal is to determine which competitors are particularly influential in your market. If you can't find market share data, try estimating the 3-5 largest competitors' market shares. Follow them on social media, understand how they communicate and how they think. Look for reasons for their success and weak links in their armor.

Their strengths can mean barriers to entry - but also opportunities, especially in our digital age. Describe the competitive advantages and the unique selling propositions (or the special customer benefits) of your largest competitors.

Determining your Market Position

What position does your business occupy in its market? You might not be able to go head-to-head with a market leader and attack its position, but if you can answer the following question, you'll have a good foot in the starting gate:

Why does (should) someone buy the product from me and not from the competition?

The following factors play an important role in positioning:

Your Assortment, Service, Price, Target Group, Presentation (online and offline), Location, and your Advertising - which includes your brand and the brand awareness your target group has with you.

Step 4. Plan Your Campaign

Facebook? TikTok? Local newspaper? YouTube? Our website? You have already thought about your target groups. Now analyze precisely where your target groups are and which content they prefer. Note: Your current channels also play a key role.

The target group to be addressed via radio advertising is different from Instagrammers.

Campaign Planning Criteria

You should already be able to sketch your ideas within the framework of a campaign plan. Ideate! Include all the options and ideas you have - maybe you won't use them on this campaign, but you will in the next one. There are no bad ideas!

You might use the following evaluation criteria for your plan: Reason, Format, User Value, Innovation, Target group, Readiness, Emotion, Shareability, Effort

Calendars

A well-developed campaign plan also includes calendar events such as public holidays, "online days" such as Doughnut Day, International Cat Day, etc. Special days that are in-line with your target group, product, and brand.

Roadmap

By setting milestones and deadlines in your campaign plan, you already have a rough roadmap. Create a timeline of the entire course of your campaign and enter essential pivot points. Don't forget to place relevant KPIs in your milestones.

Relevant deadlines that you should consider when planning your campaign can be, for example, Calendar events, Campaign and theme days, Month-end, Weekends, or duration of a set KPI.

It is worthwhile to mark milestones with corresponding dates in your roadmap for more extensive campaigns to be played out in small sections over a longer period.

Step 5. Implement Your Campaign

The next step is the implementation phase. Whether you work with external service providers or in-house people, the most important thing here is adequate time management, ongoing costs, and success measurement. In other words, managing your time well saves you money.

However, if one point gets out of hand, this is usually not a disaster. For sure, don't freak out. Experienced management can often save time or costs elsewhere so that you can ultimately work according to plan again. (It happens to the best of us.)

This step should not be difficult for you because you have planned well. However, if unforeseen things happen during the implementation phase that turns your schedule upside down, that's okay. After all, by planning your marketing campaign in detail, you can now make adjustments here and there, postpone deadlines, or -- depending on the marketing goal -- even correct the end date. You can also still call in support. The prerequisite for this is that you have planned enough buffer time. (Now, who remembers that episode in Star Trek Lower Decks?)

Step 6. Measure the Success of your Campaign

Was your effort worthwhile? At the end of the day, you should be able to answer the question of what you gained from your marketing campaign, what you did well, and how you can do a little better.

You need to evaluate the KPIs that you defined at the beginning as part of the objective. Depending on the KPI, various tools are suitable for this. You can read more about this step in the final step, Step 7 Analytics and Tracking.

Step 7. Optimize your Campaign

Optimizing an online marketing campaign is essential for success. In the process, online marketing key figures must be continuously analyzed and interpreted. If you are using ads, the budget must be monitored continuously.

Campaign performance must be continuously monitored, and regular reports created. Various analysis tools must be used for this. One of our favorites is Google Data Studio. This free tool generates online and printable reports that connect data from other tools such as Google Analytics and Google Ads - and can connect multiple websites for comparison.

Your campaign evaluation should take place regularly based on the planned campaign target figures and be an integral part of your Campaign Plan Calendar.

Step 2 -- Your Website: You do HAVE a Website, Right?

Advice on Building or Relaunching your Website

Getting Started - Requirements

Google my Business, Mailchimp, Facebook, and others offer single-page websites on their platforms. While these are good for a marketing campaign, they aren't so good for a complete website. Instead of renting space in a room with other companies, you probably want your room, or better yet, your building. So, the first thing you will need is Website Hosting.

Website hosting is offered by many providers such as GoDaddy, Ionos, or even WordPress.com. There are many providers - choose one that fits your budget and requirements. Buyer beware: you get what you pay for. If your website is eCommerce, for example, look for "managed WordPress hosting." This is key.

With your hosting company, you can order a Domain Name, Email services, storage space for your files, and often also other services like advertising and online coworking.

The most important items you receive with your Hosting are your Domain Name and server space for your website. You can install your Content Management System (CMS) on your server space and start building your website!

Our suggestion for small businesses is to use the WordPress CMS. It's the ideal, easy-to-learn, out-of-the-box system that will have your site up quickly and reliably. WordPress is a free system and comes with thousands of free themes to design your website and thousands of plugins to enhance your website's functionality. Whether you need shop functionality, plan to send newsletters, or want a cool one-page website, WordPress is perfect for small businesses. Do you need something more robust? Do you have a really big website in mind? You can also do this with WordPress! There are other free systems available, such as Drupal. You can read more about the Drupal system later on in the book.

Building a website can be much easier than putting furniture together

Installing a CMS - WordPress

CMS stands for Content Management System. It's a database. Meaning, this is a website that has quite a bit of capability as far a scaling goes. A CMS also allows you to publish blog posts. Don't look down on the humble blog; it's a significant ranking factor.

There are many different CMS on the market. Some are free; some are not. Some are easy to learn and use; others are not. If you are a small business, then you might like to use WordPress. It is free to install and use, and WordPress is used by more than 50% of the websites you see on the internet today. Larger websites might use Drupal CMS. Online Shops might use Shopify. WordPress also offers a free online shop plugin called Woocommerce.

To install WordPress, you can follow the easy steps provided by your Hosting company. Usually, WordPress installs with a few clicks and takes about 5 minutes. The WordPress installation is famously called "The 5 Minute Install." Once WordPress is installed, you can log in and begin creating your website!

When you choose a Managed WordPress Host, WordPress will already be installed. So that's nice. Managed WordPress Hosts to keep the neighborhood clean. Spending $25 a month for reliable hosting is worth the heartache it saves you. Pagely, Kinsta, WPEngine, Pressable, Site District all offer plans for any budget.

Logging in! The best website is the one you use. If you don't log in, publish blog posts, you won't know how your website works. Websites are meant to be used; they're not art pieces that collect dust.

Basic Usage - Posts, Pages, Media

Every CMS uses different terminology to describe its functions and features. WordPress has three components you will want to understand to get the ball rolling. The first is media. Media includes all the items on your website that are not text-based. Here we mean pictures, videos, files for download such as pdf and excel files, logos, charts, and audio files such as wav or mp4 files. These items can easily be uploaded and stored in WordPress's Media Library. You can add these or link to them from any page or post on your website.

A page is different from a post in a few ways. If you would like to create material connected to your menu, navigation, or be linked to other areas, you are looking at a Page. Pages typically include content that does not change. Your website developer may refer to them as "static content." Pages can also be put in a hierarchy with child/parent relationships.

A post appears on your blog. Most of us are familiar with reading blogs. We're pretty much trained to go to domain.com/blog. These posts can be events, testimonials, people, products, or anything you'd like to categorize them. This is another crucial difference between posts and pages. Posts can be categorized, and each category has an archive page. This makes navigating content much easier for the user. The better the experience, the better your SEO is. Pages and posts are both edited in similar ways. Though a page cannot have a category or tag, posts can not have "parents."

Basic Administration - The Dashboard

A good CMS offers a multitude of tools and, at first glance, may seem overwhelming. Some areas you will use every day, and some very rarely. The Dashboard, or User Interface, can be set to show only those tools you need. Website administrators (admins) see more tools than the person editing the website, for instance.

WARNING: It is almost impossible to break your website or the CMS. Relax and enjoy learning and building. But having a backup plugin isn't a bad idea either.

Every CMS offers downloadable and online step-by-step instructions on every aspect of their dashboard. WordPress is user-friendly and will notify you if any part needs to be updated or any outstanding issues or suggestions. In many cases, updates will happen automatically. If you are on a managed WordPress host, they will update things for you and notify you of any traffic spikes. (Hey, maybe people love that video you just posted on YouTube and want to buy your thing!)

WordPress also knows if you do something that might jeopardize the system and will roll back any errors. If you are editing a page or a post and make an error, WordPress offers a Revision system so you can bring back any previous version of your page. That's always nice. If you're super worried, you can always compose your blog posts in Google Docs and paste them into a new post. The WordPress Editor supports this functionality as a dream.

Pages and posts can be edited and saved in the draft format before they are published. If you're ready to publish, you can specify what day and time they will be published. Pages and posts can also be set as private, public, or password protected. How cool is that? You can even put your entire website behind a Coming Soon screen until you are happy with it being seen. WordPress admin is as easy as pie. (Well, pies get better as you make them, but who ever heard of a bad apple pie?)

Customizing Design with Themes

WordPress comes installed with three basic designs or themes. There are more than ten thousand themes, and most of them are free. You can install and switch from one theme to another with the click of a button. No programming is required to do this. With that said, with much power comes much responsibility. You can spend days looking for "the perfect theme." None exist. Choose one that is 85% of where you want to be. You'll thank us later.

Searching and installing Themes is easily done right inside your WordPress CMS. If you aren't happy with a Theme, simply deactivate it and delete it (but not before installing a new one). This is where sunk cost fallacy keeps small businesses tinkering around with their websites when their money is honestly better spent with a web developer and approving a good site. You have a business to run, right? And, as a business owner, your time is more valuable than your web developer. Do what you do with your employees, hire a good person and trust them. Launch the site and move on.

Of course, your company may want a custom design; WordPress is prepared for that. In addition to every ready-to-use Theme, WordPress offers customization options from simple click and drag and drop functions to the opportunity to upload your theme. You can buy themes, but try out the many available free themes first. Going with a Page Builder like Beaver Builder and its theme[4] is a great way to go if you want to control your design in a user-friendly way.

Within each page and post are drag-and-drop building blocks, which are part of the WordPress Editor. It is also called "Gutenberg." This standard part of WordPress allows you to display videos, build image galleries, and even build tables. You will not need to write the code; the editor does it for you. Combined with variety in theme choice, you will be able to create a unique-looking website in no time. (Seriously, if you DIY your website, stay as focused as possible. Or you could lose more time looking at every bell and whistle.)

Adding Functionality with Plugins

At this point, your website is filled with content and looks great. You even customized it to reflect your company colors and

---

[4] http://bit.ly/BuyBeaverBuilder

typography. Great job! Some things are missing, however, and WordPress has you covered. How about a contact form? SEO help? A login protection function? Perhaps even a newsletter connection to your Mailchimp account?

WordPress offers thousands of plugins that add functionality to your website. Most of these are free or freemium, meaning they have core functionality for free but add-ons or extensions that you purchase with an annual license. Plugins can be found and installed directly in WordPress, just like Themes. You can search for the function you need, browse the many plugins, install them and try them out. If you aren't happy with them, you can simply deactivate and delete them.

Maintenance -- Backups and Updates

Every good Hosting company offers you the option to backup your complete website and database on their platform. Also, you might want to back up your website piece by piece. WordPress gives you three options.

First is the database, which you can download and save on your hosting platform. The database file contains all the WordPress CMS tables and all information about the plugins, theme, and, most importantly, your content. This file will not be overly large.

Second are the files, plugins, and themes you can download and save from your web host. The file directory you want to look for is the "wp-content" folder. This file will be quite large because it contains everything you installed and uploaded onto your website.

The third item comes directly from the WordPress CMS. This is the XML file or "extended markup language" file. This is exported in your Tools section, which any Administrator will see in WordPress when they are logged in. The XML file from WordPress is a unique single-page file imported into any other WordPress website.

It contains code that is a direct copy of the content on your website. This would be the words, not the Theme or Plugin. It will be a backup of all pages, posts, and media library items. This is an essential piece of data if you would like to copy or retrieve a lost or broken website. The size of this XML file is relatively small, as it is only machine-readable code.

Security -- Passwords and Privacy

The maintenance of your website is essential - that's why you need to update and optimize your site regularly.

Why Your Website Should Be Secure

- You close security gaps
- You stay compatible with extensions and plugins
- Visitors avoid error messages
- To increase your content relevance and up-to-dateness

- Search engines prefer up-to-date websites

How Can You Stay Safe?

Back-Up Your Site Regularly

Even with a standard update, customized system files can be overwritten under certain circumstances. A regular back-up of all data is a must.

Use Secure Logins

Secure login data should be usual practice. However, the most popular password remains the numerical sequence "123456." Use a combination of:

- Lowercase letters
- Uppercase letters
- Numbers
- Symbols

Sounds complicated? Not really. The password Warr3n2008! It is not difficult to remember but would take 57,337 years and ten months to hack.

Maybe take a break and watch this video for a laugh[5].

---

[5] https://youtu.be/2tJ-NSPES9Y

Stay Up-to-Date

If you want to protect your website, you should keep yourself regularly informed about current threats and security vulnerabilities. Your hosting provider will also inform you as to essential updates of software such as PHP. Your website CMS will notify you when a theme, plugin, or the CMS itself needs to be updated. Managed WordPress hosts will do this for you. This is where the extra cost pays off.

Secure Your Site

HTTPS secures the exchange of sensitive data on your website. With the SSL key's help, data exchange between server and client takes place in encrypted form. This is an essential safeguard against a possible hack. Fortunately, this is standard practice now and is generally included with any reputable web host.

Remember: An up-to-date website helps you attract more customers. This is good for SEO.

Best Practice

Everything that goes on your website - themes, plugins, code, stylesheets, images, pdfs, videos, copy, keywords - needs to be saved on your hard drive for reference and in the event of a server error deletion. This is the backup. UpdraftPlus[6], for

---

[6] https://updraftplus.com/

example, will make a backup every night (according to how you schedule it) and save it to your Dropbox folder. That's even better. This means if your computer falls off the kayak when you're remote working, no worries, it's in the cloud. This is the backup solution Bridget uses. She's not kayaking with her computer, but you get the point.

Before each update of your CMS, plugins, or themes, make a backup of your database and files. Keep these together with your web files if an update goes sideways! Even better, hire a web developer to do this for you. Many companies offer entirely affordable maintenance packages. Bridget works with DesignFrame Solutions[7] and Press Hero[8]. Both of them have excellent options.

Every URL, customer number, license number, password, and username should be saved in a word document and kept together with your website files. Even better, save these in a cloud-based solution. If you don't have more than one backup in more than one location, you don't have a backup.

---

[7] https://designframesolutions.com/wordpress-development-services/maintenance-plans/?ref=8
[8] https://presshero.co/maintenance/

It's never fun fixing things. It's best to have a backup.

Step 2 Bonus -- The Client Worksheet

So you want to have an agency build your website. We've put together this handy worksheet to help you think about the project. This is a business plan for your website. The more information you can give the agency the better.

Each team member may have a different view of this project, so you should complete this worksheet as a group. That way, you won't miss any critical opinions or requirements. Sales will want the website to do one thing, Marketing another. The boss will have an idea, as will you. Get everybody on board!

If your site is an online shop (eCommerce), refer to that section for more tips and advice.

All About You and Your Brand / Company / Service

1. What's the name of your company and website?
2. Describe your company
3. Describe what your site will provide
4. Who are the primary contacts for this project, and what are their roles?

5. When would you like to start?

6. When does the site need to be completed?

7. What is your reason for this date? (e.g., tradeshow, product launch, vacation?)

8. What are you thinking of spending on the website project? (eg, 1-2k, 3-4k, 5k+)

What are you trying to do? What is the goal of this project?

1. What are the main reasons for wanting a (new) website

2. What are the main objectives of the website

3. What are you hoping to achieve? (increase in sales?)

4. What parts of your current site work well, and why are they successful?

5. What's not working so well?

Who are you doing it for?

1. Who's coming to your website? What are the different types of visitors to your website, and what you need to provide them with?

2. How do you think your company and the services you provide are currently seen? How about your website?

3. What are people using your site for? What will they want to do there? What features will be required?

4. Why would people choose your website instead of others?

Design Concept

1. People are coming to your new site for the first time. How do you want them to feel about your company?

2. Tell us a bit about your competition. Who are the runners and riders in your field (including their website addresses)?

3. What is good about your competitors? What isn't so good?

4. Have you seen any websites that you liked the design of? What did you like about them?

5. Let's briefly talk about content. Aside from the features we discussed above, what else do you want your website to do?

6. Do you already have an idea about which content management system you would like to use?

Tech Stuff

1. What should happen on your site regarding functionality?

2. Existing hosting or other technical barriers or expectations the agency should know about?

3. Do you have existing vendors or other services that will be migrated?

4. Will your site need to be in one or more languages?

5. Who will maintain the site? Who will manage the site? Is it a vendor or an employee?

Additional Comments

Here is your chance to add any extra information you think will be helpful to your project. Brainstorm as much as you like. Take your time. A website is built only once every three years.

Step 3 -- People's Intent: Search and SEO

What is SEO?

When people enter a search query into a search engine such as Google, they expect the search to return results (websites), completely satisfying their requirements. With the massive amount of information on the Web (enough data to fill CDs that when stacked encircle the earth 222 times12), the ambiguities of human language, flexible location and device usage, and the short-worded or incomplete queries users often enter, a thoroughly satisfying result can be wishful thinking.

Though we try our best to build artificial intelligence that is freakishly accurate, the fact is that everyone has different intent when they open a browser. They may search, but why? Are they searching for their competitors? Are they looking for a new winter coat? Why? Is it because they live in Minnesota and lost weight, or are they going on a trip to Norway?

The more we search, the more we expect instant results. Google, Bing, and the others provide this for us. Ask Alexa or Siri, where the nearest mechanic is. They'll tell you.

Search is even more complicated because people write content in different ways, often layout their websites counterproductively. In the end, Search Engines are mostly blind to both website design and our intent, among other things. Or, as Bridget likes to say, "the Internet is blind; it's the words that matter."

If you have a website, you probably want people to find it. In terms of sheer volume, this is like trying to find that PDF you saved on one of the DVDs in your collection encircling the Earth. Search Engine Optimisation (SEO) aims to ensure your website shows as high as possible in the results. This is so people can find it.

For this to happen, two things need to be considered: User Intent (what exactly is the person searching for) and Page Quality (how well the web page provides the information that is being sought).

SEO and SEA are two parts of Search Engine Marketing (SEM). SEM deals with all the measures used to position a website in the organic and paid search engines range. Search Engine Advertising (SEA) is the practice of buying ad space that appears in the search results (text ads) or on the websites of the display network (banner ads). Are that enough acronyms for you? You can market to search engines, ensure your website is technically sound with useful information, and you can purchase ads. Marketing. Search. Advertising.

How do Search Engines Work?

If you spend time optimizing your website for Search Engines, it helps to understand how they work.

Search Engines have four basic functions:

- To Crawl the internet,
- to Create an index,
- to Calculate relevance and rankings of pages;
- and to Provide a list of results.

Search Engines cannot see your beautiful website design and do not care how much effort you spent deciding your corporate colors. Instead, they must interpret your website's content – much like a reader must interpret the meaning of something they are reading.

Search Engines have no inherent quality or notability control function or a way to discover and make visible the great content available on the web. Only people can do that – at the moment anyway.

The internet is a big place. It's not always easy to find what you're looking for. SEO can help us make it easier for people to find what we want to show them.

How Can I Help Search Engines Find My Website?

When a user enters a search query, the Search Engine scrambles in microseconds to find websites and content that it believes might be what they want to see. Think back again on those two fundamental aspects: User Intent (what is the user looking for) and Page Quality (how easily your website makes the content people are looking for available).

Factors that can assist a Search Engine in delivering your website to the list of results include:

- Relevance: How closely is your page's content to the intent of the user who made the search query?

- Authority: is your page or domain a popular authority? Are you a valid source of information?

- Scope and Utility: does your page recognize the intent of the user?

- Page Presentation: is your website professional-looking, organized, and thorough?

- Market: is your website relevant to the specific region of the user's search query?

- Language: is your website related to the market and query?

- Location: is your website suitable for the user's location requirement or a search?

- Freshness: much like relevance – is your website offering up-to-date content?

That's a Lot of Words. Can We Have Some Numbers Now?[9]

Google manages 65% of all searches on the internet, and over 4 Billion Google searches occur on average each month.

Twenty percent of search queries are for local information. Yes, your website must have up-to-date and correct information like hours, phone, and addresses.

- Position 1 in the search results receives almost 30% of the clicks.

- Position 2 receives about 15%.

- Position 3 receives about 11%.

- Position 4 about 8% and everything else less than 8% of all clicks.

You Made this Up, Didn't You? What does Google Suggest?

Make your pages and website for people – for your target market. Don't build your websites solely for Search Engines.

- Do not disappoint your users.

- Don't try to trick Search Engines with fake or distracting content or sites.

- Structure your website using a clear system of content (hierarchy) and text links.

- Every page should be reachable within one click via a text link.

- Create a useful, informative, relevant website.

- Provide content that is clear and concise.

---

[9] *https://www.sistrix.com/blog/why-almost-everything-you-knew-about-google-ctr-is-no-longer-valid/.

And Something Else – Don't Forget Context

In addition to User Intent and Page Quality, the secret to understanding a search query and delivering the correct result is Context. A meaningful analysis of a user's context requires not only an understanding of the user's goals but also of their behavior:

- what are they doing (carrying food? driving? in a meeting?),
- how do they feel (lousy day? great day? fired? in love?);
- and, what are they capable of at the moment of searching (mobile? one hand? two?)

Whether people see and respond to your content depends as much on understanding their goals as it does on their context. We must make our website accessible to them – regardless of whether they are searching on their phone in the car or searching on their desktop in the office.

Suppose the average visitor spends 137 seconds on your website. In that case, it's not a nicety to deliver appealing, relevant, and consistent website content – it's a necessity if you want your website to be found.

About Voice Search

Do you have a personal assistant-like device? An Alexa or a Siri – or a Judi or a Bob, I don't know. The days of our searching the internet for websites by typing into Google are numbered. Why type when we can talk?

Voice-activated content refers to content delivered via smart speakers, assistants such as Amazon Alexa, Siri, Google Home, and other smart devices. According to Statista,[10] about three billion digital voice assistants are being used around the world. By 2023 that number could reach eight billion – so about the same number of voice assistants as people.

Open your windows, and you'll hear neighbors talking to their assistants.

"Alexa, where can I find the closest florist?"

"Siri, who won the World Series in 1945?"

Now, put the power of voice search into your Content Marketing strategy. Content Marketing involves creating and sharing material that, while not explicitly promoting a brand, is intended to stimulate interest in its products or services. Comic books, advertorials, cartoons – Content Marketing has been around for decades. Now it can be delivered at the touch of your finger-tips – or in this case, at the tip of your tongue.

Voice Content Marketing is a strategy that encourages you to answer questions your customers may have. The more useful your website is to your customer, the better your SEO will be. It's that simple. Two years ago, all of the experts predicted it as

---

[10] Published by Statista Research Department, Feb 19, 2020

the new way to market as if we're not ready. We're already here.

When's the last time you talked to your voice assistant? Did you ask her questions? Did she answer you? Were the results from a website? That's voice content marketing.

Alexa Skills

Check out Alexa Skills[11]. Your company should get in on this. It's like Dash Buttons used to be before Amazon stopped them in the winter of 2018.

Voice Search and You

Don't worry; voice search is easy to grasp. It's necessary to make your Content Marketing effective. While it may be a bit scary, it fits into our semantic and contextual search patterns nicely, but with much less typing. (And who doesn't like less typing, right?) This is important because we speak far more casually than we type. This means reduced wordiness and increased semantics.

Instead of typing in "inexpensive family holidays in Spain with hotel and car rental" to get all of Google's pistons firing, I might just say, "Alexa, where can we go in Spain that's cheap?" This doesn't work yet because not enough websites are set up for

---

[11] www.amazon.com/alexa-skills/b/?ie=UTF8&node=13727921011&ref_=topnav_storetab_a2s

voice search, and we are still using our fingers to ask Google - but you get my meaning. One day voice will replace the keyboard or mobile search.

Voice Search works like this. When you ask your assistant to look for something, it will read out the information found in the rich snippets from your website, which appear in Google search results. We call this the meta description.

Make sure your website:

- is optimized for local search (sometimes called mobile search),
- uses the schema.org protocol for rich snippets (the Yoast SEO plugin does),
- loads quickly;
- and is relevant.

We can type about 40 words a minute, but we can speak three times as many. We have the mental capacity to understand four hundred words a minute. Voice search isn't the future. Voice search is now.

Voice Search -- The Future is Now

Think about it. As Alexa learns what we want and what our family wants based on the previous months' worth of searches and requests, she will no longer be delivering rich snippets. She may one day be providing this result to my query on cheap family holidays in sunny Spain:

"I have found three websites for cheap family holidays in Spain, but based on your current bank balance and the searches of your family, might I suggest a cheap family holiday in Seattle instead? Your wife googled Pike Street Market 16 times last month. Your children want to learn more about Whales as well. I have booked your trip. By the way, I hear from your coffee machine that you are low on coffee, and your copy of "The University Club – A Campus Affair" will arrive today. Have a nice vacation!"

What about Social Media and SEO?

When factoring in your social media efforts into your SEO plan, it comes down to your content's purpose. Is it to be shared on social media or to be found on Google or both?

Google uses Schema.org structured data to build rich-data results for its search. If you want to optimize for Google, Bing, and other search engines, use the Schema.org markup.

Both formats are part of the Yoast SEO plugin for WordPress. Here is an example of a page from my website with the Schema.org markup:

<div class="schema-faq wp-block-yoast-faq-block">

<div class="schema-faq-section" id="faq-question-1580541566541">What is the Biggest Problem in SEO?

<p class="schema-faq-answer">The biggest problem in SEO is that websites are built by people, but websites are indexed by machines.</p>

</div></div>

Additionally, Facebook Open Graph (OG) markup needs to be added if you want to turn your content into a social object. Twitter, LinkedIn, and the rest all defer to Open Graph. It's

Facebook's tool, and it's their rules on their playground. Just as Google rules search, Facebook rules social.

Here is the same page with additional OG markup:

<meta property="og:url" content="https://warrenlainenaida.net/" />

<meta property="og:site_name" content="Warren Laine-Naida" />

Next Steps -- Search Intent Assignments

- Take out a pen and paper and write down the last thing you searched for. If you can't think of that, then search for "double-hung windows in San Antonio, Texas" or "pizza near me."

- What was the reason you searched for that item?

- How difficult was it to find the answer you were looking for?

- How did you feel while reading the websites?

- Did anything frustrate you?

- What did you like about the sites you found?

- How does this experience cause you to think differently about your website and content marketing?

SEO and Search: Creating your SEO Plan

We can't stress enough the importance of Search Engine Optimisation to the success of your online marketing. If people can't find you, they can't buy from you. It's that simple. A good SEO plan is not complicated, but it will take time and a budget. If you plan to do it yourself, it will also require a good understanding of who your customers are and what they want.

Remember, 70% of the clicks on Google are unpaid, organic results, while 30% are paid search ads. So, it pays, pun intended, to spend most of your time working on your SEO game.

Where Do I Start?

There are three main steps to your SEO Plan:

1. Target customers and their objectives or needs

2. Target search intent. Meaning, the keywords and search phrases they use

3. An analysis of your website, social media, and online ads

What If I Can't Do This?

Before you begin, you might like to print the following reminders out and hang them on your wall. In moments of confusion or stress, they will help you get back in the game!

***

There are **no** quick fixes. SEO, like any form of good marketing, is **a long game**.

Be Realistic with your expectations; think about **solutions** to problems rather than gimmicks. Be prepared to **Adapt and Test** your SEO to technical, seasonal, and market changes.

SEO is a **mixture of marketing and psychology**. It can be both fun and educational to discover what drives people to your website.

People search with intent. They are looking to **find something**, **complete a transaction**, or **get information**. Banner or display advertising is passive. It can distract you - and no one purposely looks for an advertisement.

***

SEO Step One -- Who are your Target Customers, and what are their Objectives or Needs?

You might be surprised to learn that your target customers are not only potential customers. You should be thinking about existing customers and your employees who are natural influencers for your brand. What do they want? What problem does your product or service solve? How does it make their life better? How much does it cost? Where can they get it?

SEO Marketing

Breaking your target customers down into specific groups will assist you in your SEO planning.

- Demographic features - age, income, gender, interests, language

- Geographic features - local, specific city, neighborhood, country, postal code

- Tastes and Trends - yuppies, generation Z, fashion tastes

- Buying behavior - coupon cutters, bulk buyers, price over quality

SEO Psychology

Think about your target customer's goals and priorities. What do they really want? (We know you're singing the Spice Girls song right now. We know "what you want, what you really, really want." That's knowing your customer.)

Think about their pain points. What frustrates them, and how can you solve that problem? How will you tackle that in their product and service, and how your website is set up. Will selling on social media solve it? Maybe offering free local delivery is the solution.

Think about what excites your customers. What opportunities does this present you to DELIGHT them?

SEO Step Two -- Search Intent and the Keywords and Search Phrases We Use

Put yourself in your target customer's shoes. Think about how you search for things that you want. What words or groups of words do users use to search for your products or services? Open Google and search for something you want or a problem you have. Look at your search query. Is it a single keyword? Is it two keywords? Probably not. People don't search like that.

Your target customers are searching using questions and multiple words. Use these words and phrases in your website copy to help Google and your target customers find you faster! Google is concerned about one thing - that people find RELEVANT results for their search.

Suppose someone searches for "Summer Penny Loafers on sale in San Antonio" and your shoe store is in that city, and your website has the copy "Come into our San Antonio store this week for our big Summer sale on Penny Loafers." In that case, Google will see that as a very relevant result to show them.

Does it feel like a lot of words? Are you wondering who searches like that? Well, everyone! Google tells us that half of the searches use two to three words. HALF! That means the other half uses four words or more. We have grown used to asking Google questions and giving as much information as possible for the best result to our search. (We just talked about voice search, remember?)

Many, many people search Google by asking a question.[12] "How to register to vote?", "What is my IP?", "How do I make pancakes?", "How do I lower my blood pressure?", "Where can I find good legal advice?" ...

Based on this information, you can edit the copy on your website to read:

"**How much** is our **Summer Sale Penny Loafers**? **Why** should you have a pair? **Where** can you buy them? Join us **all this week** in our **San Antonio store on Main street** and walk out in a **comfortable** pair for **15% off**!"

Easy peasy lemon squeezy and a ready customer is clicking on your snippet!.

Need a helping hand here?

- Open Google and type in a question. Scroll down. See? Google offers questions similar to your own that others are asking. Aha!

- You can use Google's Keyword Tool to begin keyword research to learn what your customers are searching for.

- Google Trends also offers help with what search terms are trending.

- Check your Social Media account. Listen to what people are talking about and why.

---

[12] https://www.mondovo.com/keywords/most-asked-questions-on-google

SEO Step Three -- Analyse your Website, Social Media, and Online Ads

The third and final step of your SEO plan is the most time-consuming, so we would advise you to break it down into smaller tasks. We've done that below. Tackling it all in one go might be overwhelming. We don't want you to give up before you start.

Now that you have a good idea of who your customers are, where they live, their problems and priorities, and which key phrases can be used on your website, the next step is to take a look at your website itself.

"If people love your website, then Google loves your website."

Combined, your relevant, safe, and important website is judged by how edible it is. Yes, you read that correctly. Google looks at your EAT quality: Expertise, Authority, and Trust.

Google has more than 200 ranking factors deciding which website appears in which order in the search results. It changes its search algorithm 500 times a year. Google wants people to find what they are looking for.

Google will show your website higher up in the search results because you have RELEVANT website copy that answers people's queries. Google wants to know two other things.

Google wants to know that your website is SAFE. Is it broken? Is it out of date? Is it a security risk? Does it work on mobile phones? Google also wants to know how IMPORTANT your website is. Does it have links from other websites? Are you active on social media? Do you have customer reviews?

That's what we're going to do now -- check to see that your website is safe and important!

Checking Under the Hood of Your Website

Let's begin with a review of your website. You can do this using free online tools.

Security of your website

Data protection, cookies, SSL certificate, and much more.

https://webbkoll.dataskydd.net

Speed of your website

The faster it is, the more Google will like it. Especially for mobile.

https://developers.google.com/speed/pagespeed/insights

Optimize Website Images

Overly large images take longer to load. Make them smaller.

https://tinypng.com

Look at your website like the Google bots do

This tool is installed on your computer. It maps your website much as the Google bots do.Is something missing? Here you'll get an excellent overview:

https://www.screamingfrog.co.uk/seo-spider

Missing Keywords?

Google ads give you suggestions on which keywords fit your ads, and you can use these keywords to optimize your website copy. Do not use keywords indiscriminately. That would be keyword stuffing and is frowned upon by Google in the extreme. Keywords should be relevant to your copy and the intent of the visitor.

https://ads.google.com/intl/de_de/home/tools/keyword-planner

Check the SEO Score of Your Website

To optimize your website for Search Engines, break down the task into three parts:

- On-Page Optimisation (SEO to do with the pages, posts, and media on your website)

- Off-Page Optimisation (SEO to do with your social media, reviews, and links to your site)

- And Technical Optimisation (SEO to do with the performance and structure of your site)

On-Page Optimization (what is on your website)

Optimizing the content and copy of your website takes time and is never finished. A website is organic; the content changes with your customers' trends and needs and the marketplace. The closer you are in tune with your customers, the better you will optimize your website's content. The result will be a website that is found and visited more often! Since a website isn't print, you can edit the copy once you learn about your customers. Don't do too much editing at once, however, or you won't know what changes helped.

Meta Tags for Title and Description

Google looks at the title and description of your page to understand what the page is about. It also looks at the main headline title (h1) and the headline subtitles (h2) to understand what information appears on your page. The page title and description are found at the head of your page. The h1 and h2 are located in the body of your page. Every page has only one headline (h1) but as many subtitles (h2) as necessary.

<title>Donut King | Los Angeles</title>

<meta property="og:description" content="Donut King. Fresh Donuts made daily!" />

<h1>Our Daily Favorites</h1>

<h2>Chocolate Glazed</h2>

Elements for Headings

Headings and titles are attention grabbers for humans but also need to provide valuable information for Google. Very often, they ask a question which is then answered in the following paragraph. Writing great, eye-catching titles does not come immediately, but you will learn how to create the perfect headings as you go along.

One trick to use is the formula (# + adjective + "what it is" + the impact). For example, compare these two headlines:

- Chocolate Glazed Donuts!
- 6 Delicious Chocolate Donuts to Please Your Hungry Family!

Which headline would you more likely notice?

The caveat here is that you don't want your headings to be clickbait either. So don't promise something you don't deliver. Bridget loves using "people also ask" from a Google search as her trick to outline the page or blog post. There's no better insight into search intent than to use the suggestion from Google.

Images and Alt Tags

Every image, pdf, or video that you upload to your website's media library should be named to match your brand and the function it has on your site. This benefits your SEO and accessibility while protecting you from having your images used without considering your copyright.

Poor practice: <img src="donuts.jpg" alt="donuts">

Best practice: <img src="donut-king-chocolate-donuts.jpg" alt="These chocolate donuts are baked fresh daily in our Los Angeles stores.">

The title, description, and alt tags of all media can be set when uploaded into your media database via WordPress. Optimize your images for size and name the file correctly BEFORE you upload them. This will save you a lot of headaches later. You're welcome.

A 1 MB image is far too large to be used on your website. It will take longer to load, and most people are looking at your website on a desktop, tablet, or phone - not on a TV screen.

Formats: Photos: jpegs Graphics: pngs Videos: mp4s Sizes: 1280x720 pixels is the most common size of images. Some slider images are 1920 pixels. That should be your maximum width.

Image data size: images should be no larger than 300k

Website Copy

A good landing page is essential if you want to connect with your audience. Poor landing pages disappoint visitors, resulting in a high bounce rate - they come, they see, they leave! If you want to structure your pages and write website copy that connects with people, you need to understand why they came to your website - and deliver it to them within 30 seconds!

It may seem frustrating and kind of like a catch 22. I can't write the content until I know what they want, but I can't know what they want unless I have a page? We go into more depth in our section on Landing Pages, so don't worry.

Here's the thing. It's just a website. Write something. Publish it. Look at your Google analytics and see how many hits it gets. If people are still asking questions, add some of those answers to that page. We have this concept that a website is a brochure. That goes back to the days of print (not that they're dead). So, we think the website should never be edited. It's simply not true. Don't keep changing the design; edit the words.

Internal Link Structure

Internal linking is a great way to optimize your website structure and improve your SEO. Find pages and articles on your website discussing the same topic, then link to that post. It might feel like you're quoting yourself. It's okay. You're the expert; that's why the customer is on your site. What you're doing is creating hospitality. You're making it easy for the visitor to explore your site easily. If they're frustrated, they will bounce.

Think of this as a journey with the intent of keeping visitors on your website. You do this by handing them a map, to some extent. Except they don't realize they've spent 30 minutes reading on your site until their phone rings.

Example:

> *Our chocolate donuts are baked each day with the <u>finest local ingredients</u> (link to a page with these ingredients as a backlink to your suppliers). The donuts are packed and delivered to some of your <u>favorite coffee shops</u>! (Link here to a page where these coffee shops are listed and linked with why you like them so much.)*

Navigation (Menu) Names and Structure

We often create our navigation menu from an internal perspective. This often leaves visitors confused as to what we mean by "Structure," "Products," or "Services." Since your audience isn't searching for "products" or "services," navigation with these labels won't help.

At the same time, most people are used to looking for your "blog," "contact us," and "about" pages. If people can't find the information they're looking for, they bounce. Make sure your menus make sense. You can have more than one!

Off-Page Optimization (links to your website through Social Media and other Press)

Backlinks - Links to Your Website

Backlinks are an important SEO ranking factor. If you want to get more Google traffic for your website, backlinks are key. Talk with partners, link with suppliers, write posts about your products and those of your partners. Think of how you would promote and connect with real people and backlink your website with others. A list of links is not the way to go. That was yesterday.

When you ask, don't be spammy about it either. There's a nuance and a polite way to ask.

Targeted Content

Who are you targeting? What are they looking for? Where are they? Think about the last news article you read. Did you read it to the end? Did it inspire you to check facts or to read more about the subject? If it did, the content spoke to you. You were the target audience.

Think about what information you can share on social media and include on your website. This will create the same effect for your target customer. Content can also be written to be relevant according to the season and trends.

Trending on Social Media:

Drinking coffee and eating chocolate in a moderate amount can improve heart health.

Your Response:

A blog article about the quality and portion size of your coffee and chocolate glazed donuts. You have a special on small coffees and miniature chocolate glazed donuts to promote heart health.

Promote On Social Media

What does social media have to do with search engine results? Everything. Well, a lot. If you Google a person's name, you will likely see in the search results a link to their Twitter, Linkedin, and Facebook pages. Suppose you search for images, you are often given links to Pinterest. Google loves social media, too!

Writing about your website and posting on Facebook is not enough. Again, your posts should speak to your target customer. It should be about a relevant and trending topic. Most importantly, social media, as you have already read, is about having a conversation. Write your posts with a question in mind. Get people talking. Be the center of the conversation. It's just like networking.

Why Social Media is important to your SEO:

- Social Media: Link potential to your website
- Google indexes tweets
- Personalization of search results
- The volume of search results
- Social Signals: Brand Signals
- Building relationships
- Building Trust

Content Marketing

Sometimes we create content, the sole purpose of which is to promote a product. Comic books are a perfect example, as are modern cartoons and breakfast cereals. Those free magazines you get at the store with coupons and free advice? They're an example of content marketing.

Content Marketing and SEO go hand-in-hand. They overlap. SEO makes demands, and Content marketing fulfills them. Think of it as a conversation between two people. At the center of Content Marketing is the idea of giving extra value to your customers. Think about our Donut Store. How can we give extra value to our visitors? How about a free recipe?

Suggested Content Marketing post for the DonutKing Website:

Five Yummy Donuts to Eat On the Road

We all love donuts, though we don't always admit it! Sometimes, the sprinkles, coconut, nuts, and sugar make it a messy treat for our road trip. To solve this messy conundrum, we've created five "topping free" donuts -- just for you.

Chocolate, Strawberry Swirl, Maple, Sour Blueberry, Plain Old Fashioned - Click here to order!

Like our new Sour Blueberry Donut? Scroll down for our easy-to-make recipe!

Other forms of Content Marketing include blog posts that may also contain: videos, tutorials, advice pages, infographics, games, surveys, studies, ebooks, and whitepapers. Whitepapers and ebooks are great lead generation tools. Oh yeah, want to sign up for our list? We'll give you a free ebook!

Google My Business

Google offers every business a free tool to help promote themselves. Free posts, product placement, offers, maps, contact information, and customer reviews appear on the organic search page free of charge!

When you search for a business on Google, you often find it appearing on the results' top right-hand side. Cool, right? That's Google My Business. The GMB tool is the middle ground between search and social media and is often displayed on their maps!

Have you asked Siri or Alexa to find "an Italian place near me?" That GMB listing helps -- especially on mobile. You should optimize your listing as well.

Your Google My Business account is much more than just a business listing. With your free business profile, you can easily reach new customers via Google Maps and Google Search.

Why are you still here? Register today![13]

Technical SEO (how your website works)

Choose the Correct Domain

Your domain name (URL) is the first thing people see. Now that websites have been around for the better part of 25 years, many of those domain names are taken. Domain names should be part of your branding strategy. If you're not known in your area, someone could think that donutking.com is a donut vending machine. (Wait. They have those?) In contrast, donutking-donutshops.com tells the visitor that you are a donut shop.

A domain consisting of only of the company name: donutking.com

A domain consisting only of the keyword: donutshops.com

A domain consisting of a mixture of company name and keyword: donutking-donutshops.com

[13] https://www.google.com/business

Subdomains vs. Subfolders

Deciding on which you choose to incorporate your content depends on a variety of factors. Consider usability and your strategic objective, and then decide on the optimal variant. Meaning, who is your audience, and what would they expect? This way, you can achieve the best results for on-page search engine optimization until the end.

donutking-donutshops.com/delivery or delivery.donutking-donutshops.com

Both function just as well. However, most users know that the delivery would come after your domain. They know you're donutking-donutshops.com, so probably deliver is "/delivery." On the other hand, if you are a WordPress plugin, other developers would presume your documentation would be a subdomain: docs.domainname.com. No matter which section of this book you're in, we're probably going to say "know your audience" a few times. #SorryNotSorry

A directory primarily benefits the domain, not the blog itself -- but that's exactly the reason for the blog. Blog posts get backlinks. These are ranking factors for the blog. Subdomains spread the power to the rest of the domain but not as much. A directory passes on more power; I have tested this countless times.

A subdomain would make sense for landing pages featured in advertising campaigns - Summer Sale, Winter Clearance, Our

Special Service - which might otherwise threaten to take over the domain keywords. For example, if a company has its employees blog about vacations, then a subdomain would be better for almost all industries. The hotel and vacation industries could benefit.

Web Host

To ensure the accessibility and speed of your website, server hosting must have the right infrastructure. This not only involves the use of high-quality hardware components from brand manufacturers for the individual dedicated servers and virtual servers but above all for the components used in the data center infrastructure. For these reasons, it's important to use a reputable and reliable hosting provider. Spoiler Alert: the right hosting provider will also save you money!

Shop and compare hosting providers for their price, reliability, bandwidth, location, storage, performance, support, features, and ratings. If you're spending less than $25/month on your web hosting, you will lose some of these features. If any sales happen on your site (eCommerce), we highly recommend a Managed WordPress host.

HTML vs. CMS

CMS is content-focused. Content answers questions. A CMS is a database. HTML sites are great if your website is one page. Then again, if your website is one page, you're going to have a challenging time ranking.

Google prefers a database. Why? More data means more answers to their users. It is to their advantage for Google to provide answers users are searching for.

If you like the speed of HTML and the organization and ranking of a CMS, then consider a static generator. There are so many options in the JAMstack space, including Strattic.com and GetShifter.io. These static site generators essentially function as your host. Like anything, the choice depends upon your business goals and knowing your audience (see what we did there?).

Page Speed and Mobile Friendliness

One of the most important factors of SEO is usability -- the user-friendliness of a website for visitors. After clicking on the search results link, one of the most important usability factors becomes noticeable: page load. Google has been saying for years that page speed has an impact on the ranking of websites. A fast website means a modern, minimal, and user-friendly website. (Even if people don't have AT&T's new 5G network.)

Mobile-first design means that the mobile version is used for ranking - even on the desktop. The search engine giant launched its Mobile-First Index, first announced in 2018. If your target customer is searching for a product using their mobile device, and your website is not mobile-friendly, you will not appear in the search results. Why? Because your website is not relevant or useful to the person searching.

Remember, iPads and tablets are mobile devices. (Mind blown, right?)

Robots.txt and .htaccess file

The Robots.txt file permits Google and other bots to crawl your site. Secure your site and tell Google about missing and moved pages in your .htaccess file.

Not excited about making changes in these files? No worries. You can do this in your SEO plugin very easily. Yoast and Rank Math has great SEO plugins for free, and both have reasonable Pro versions. It's worth upgrading.

301 Redirects

If you plan to relaunch your website or a page that once but no longer exists, you can set up a 301 redirect to the new page in your .htaccess file. You can tell Google that this page no longer exists and is not being redirected as well. If a visitor goes to this old URL, they will be automatically redirected to the page's new URL.

Old website page: donutking-donutshops.com/donutholes

New website page: donutking-donutshops.com/donut-holes

As this would appear in your .htaccess file
Redirect 301 /donut holes https://donutking-donutshops.com/donut-holes

Not excited about making changes in your htaccess file? No worries. You can do this in your Yoast SEO plugin very easily.

404 Errors

No one likes landing on a 404 "page not found." Well, sometimes your 404 pages can be funny and clever. To make this experience good for your user, have a bit of fun. Make your 404 pages humorous. You can do this easily with Beaver Builder[14]. Use it as an opportunity to list the top pages people look for on your website and a search field.

If you have products or pages that are often misspelled, redirect these to the correct page to avoid a 404. This goes as well for pages that you had on your old website, which no longer exist.

Congratulations!

Wow. That was a lot. SEO is one of the most important parts of your online marketing, so the time you have spent here is time well-invested.

We gave you the best overview of each item possible, but every section deserves a small book of its own. Use these recommendations as to the first step in mastering the art of Search Engine Optimisation.

Remember, your market always changes; customers change, trends change, and technology changes. Pencil-in an SEO

---

[14] http://bit.ly/BuyBeaverBuilder

checkup once a quarter. That way, your hard work will only need a small polish, instead of a huge clean!

Landing Pages 101

What Is a Landing Page?

A landing page is a page on your website designed to convert visitors into leads. It is different from other pages on your website that are minimal with one purpose: the call to action.

Your landing page shouldn't include a sidebar, navigation, or unnecessary text. A call to action can be a form that allows you to capture a visitor's information in exchange for the desired offer. That form should be unique to your landing page. The landing page's CTA can also be a "buy now" button. The sole purpose of the landing page is to convert visitors into leads or customers. You can have a mix of lead generation and commerce landing pages, too.

Once you start creating these unique pages which are not in your website's main navigation, you'll get the hang of it.

How Do Landing Pages Work?

Use the AIDA principle to understand how your landing page works and why it's important. AIDA stands for Attention, Interest, Desire, and Action.

- Attention: The customer becomes aware of a product or brand (usually through advertising or social media).

- Interest: The customer becomes interested in the product benefits & how the product fits their lifestyle.

- Desire: The customer develops a favorable disposition towards the product.

- Action: The customer makes a purchase.

The Conversion Process

The landing page is the main component of the conversion process, but it is one of three parts that will make your conversion successful.

Call to Action (CTA): A CTA (post, ad, or link) prompts your visitors to click. On landing pages, CTAs tell the visitor where they should click to access the offer. CTAs can also be found on other pages of your website.

Landing Page: The landing page itself is home to the form that a visitor fills out to access the offer. Once the form is submitted, a visitor should be redirected to a "thank you" page.

Thank You, Page: Thank you pages can include a further CTA to continue the conversion process and move the lead down the marketing funnel with other offers. Eachthank you page should be unique to a landing page.

Landing pages and thank you pages are like peanut butter and jelly. They go together and should always be a unique pair. You'll be glad you did this later when you set up Goals in Google Analytics.

TEST DRIVE? CLICK HERE

Great Landing Pages are concise and uncluttered.

Building a Great Landing Page

Here are some best practices for building a solid landing page:

A Compelling Headline

The headline answers the need of the customer. It explains why they are there, and it is the first thing they see when they get to your landing page.

State Your Offer

Make the value to the visitor clear. You have about 3-5 seconds for someone to decide if they want to stay on your landing page. If they come from a search or an ad, you need to convince them to stay on the page quickly. Use clear language.

Build the Form

Collect just as much information as you need for the lead. Don't overcomplicate it. Most of the time, a name and email are enough. You will need to ensure you have a data protection note on your forms. Users must confirm their agreement that you can use the information they provide in the form for the purpose it is being collected. (See more about this topic in our Legal Section)

Remove Distractions

When building a landing page, you want to remove any opportunity for your visitor to be distracted from your offer. This includes your main navigation and sidebars.

Videos and Images

Images allow the visitor to picture themselves in the shot. We call this image the "hero shot." The addition of video also serves to keep the visitor on your page longer. An image and a video together can increase your page retention by as much as six times over a page without them.

Provide Reviews

Reviews add a level of trust to your landing page. Who else bought your product? Customer ratings are also good here if longer testimonials are not available.

Analyze the Results

Once your campaign is up and running, and traffic is being driven to your page, check the results of your landing pages frequently.

If you make changes to your landing pages (e.g., copy, images, form fields), be sure to change one thing at a time and test the results.

If you change multiple things at once and there is a sudden drop or increase in responses, you won't know what you did to cause this.

Step 4 -- Be In The Conversation: Social Media

Social media isn't a nice-to-have; it's a must-have. Without social media, your brand will be missing one of the pillars of SEO. Furthermore, you'll lose insight into your customers and your target market.

What we would like to break through in this chapter is the notion that social media is a frivolous activity or a waste of time. Bridget will never forget how her former boss thought I was only tweeting about her lunch. But business comes in through social media as a channel. Why? Because it's where people are.

Where Do People Do Business?

Whether it was at the city gates as we read in Biblical texts, or the Roman baths, or in the Ottoman coffee house revolution that fueled the Age of Enlightenment, business was done in gathering places. This level playing field allowed ideas to flow and why those in power tried to stop fake news.

> "On June 12, 1672, Charles II proclaimed to 'Restrain the Spreading of False News, and Licentious Talking of

Matters of State and Government,' which read in part: 'men have assumed to themselves a liberty, not only in Coffee-houses but other Places and Meetings, both public and private, to censure and defame the proceedings of State by speaking evil of things they understand not.'" History.com (Pearce Rotondi)

Later, business was done in pubs and gentlemen's clubs (*not that kind, the kind where they smoked cigars and drank brandy*). In the 1980s, deals were made on the golf course. Many of these locations are still venues for business meetings. Only middle management likes a conference room and even then formalizes deals made in other areas. They're not called "backroom deals" for nothing.

Why? Gathering places facilitate conversations. You meet people, talk shop, and ideas collide. It starts with small talk and grows in trust over time.

It's easy to forget that we humans are social animals. We need to be around other people. We need that interaction. So when your employee is online, you may think she is wasting time. She may be marketing your business despite you. But that would be another book.

For now, we ask that you would believe -- for the sake of this chapter if not for the future of your own business -- that social gatherings are the places where business is done.

What is Social Media?

The term "social media" is more simple than we think -- mainly because of our fear of tech. Social media is simply a venue for people to gather and interact with one another. It's a place to discover community, find solutions, and entertain yourself. It just happens to be online instead of the coffee house.

"Social" is the behavior. "Media" is the platform. Read that again.

So many businesses simply publish on media and forget to be social. This is where you, as a small business, have a great opportunity on social media. Because large businesses ignore people and essentially forfeit the game, you have opportunities to win those customers.

How Do You Win Customers Online?

This is where the conversation comes in. You win customers online by being the first, engaging with people where they are, and staying top-of-mind.

The best way to win customers online is to start a conversation. Over time, you build a relationship. Front the relationship, that person either is your customer or refers people to you. As you continue the conversation online, you maintain loyalty online.

Customers no longer see you as a small business that can't handle their project; you're more available for customer service. This is how social media levels the playing field for your small business.

What Is the Timeline for Social Media Success?

Ah, the timeline. Social media isn't a quick fix for bad marketing. It doesn't rescue a boat going down. Social media success is a long game -- just like most relationship-dependent businesses. Once it all clicks, you will be bummed you didn't kick and scream the whole time. We promise.

Realistically, you should start seeing a lift in website visits in the first three months and attributable sales in the first six. Now, this all depends on how you track leads. If someone comes into Donut King, our hearty example, and they are not asked, "How did you hear about us?" then you will not know -- unless there is a coupon on Instagram or something.

Key reasons to participate in social media:

1. Gain Customer Insight
2. Starting the Conversation
3. Build a Relationship
4. Maintain Loyalty

5. Tell People What You Do

Gain Customer Insight

What do your customers want, what delights them? We've talked a lot about customer delight and audience insight in this book so far. Why do we bring it up again? It's simple. Many small businesses believe they need formal market research. Maybe your competitors have it. Or maybe they don't. Either way, you need to understand your customers.

Social media gives small businesses access to the conversations that people are having about you. Your customers either love you or hate you. Worse? They're agnostic. Yikes. If you can't remember the maple bar, was it very good? To compete, we have to be memorable. That's where customer delight comes in.

All-day, every day people are posting on social media. By spending time online, we have access to who they are. Not in a creepy way. Eeww. But we will know if they drink Diet Coke or Diet Dr. Pepper. We will understand if they prefer to go fishing or kayaking. We know what news stations they like and which websites they read. This allows us to understand how to reach our customers.

If businesses and organizations can identify and access those individuals and steer the trends set in motion, they have a ready customer in waiting.

For example, if our new tequila is marketed to the 30 and under crowd, we can read what they're posting on Twitter, Instagram, and TikTok. This will show us which brands they like. Knowing that, for example, they love Have'a Corn Chips. Reaching out to Have'a may yield a good opportunity to comarket your tequila. Because your strategy rides on the coattails of another brand, you get invited as a VIP of sorts into their party.

Maybe your business offers cleaning services. Traditionally, your client base is busy moms. Well, they've sort of aged out of needing your services. The kids are gone, and they vacuum their house while making funny TikTok videos. So, how do you get more business?

Do a bit of research. Search for "mommy and me" groups. Search for keywords like "diapers" or "making baby food." If you know moms who are in their 20's, you have market insight. Maybe they're staying home and living on one income. But they still want help cleaning their homes. It's not out of the question since they grew up with concierge apps doing things for them from Uber to DoorDash to Drizzly. How do you reach them?

You do more research. What co-marketing opportunities present themselves? Are they having wine delivered for book club night? Maybe you offer a discount for the first cleaning -- and promise their home will be ready for their turn to host the mom's chardonnay book club. Perhaps your social media images will use photos you found on Unsplash of young moms laughing. They're happy because their homes are cleaned. You get it.

Starting the Conversation

Starting the conversation with your customers or target audience is easily achieved on social media. Maybe you don't have Brittney's social account to comment on her posts (and that could be odd), but you're creating an environment that allows people to speak to you. That next level of customer service is available.

Social media is hospitality -- but online. Not every social media platform allows for a reciprocal relationship between a person and a brand. For example, Facebook profiles can like Facebook Pages. Pages cannot send a friend request to a profile. It goes against Facebook's Terms of Service (TOS) for brands to have profiles. This is a measure to protect the privacy of users.

So, how can a brand start a conversation on Facebook? One way is to optimize your Facebook Page so that they can find you in search. Secondly, post information that is helpful and creates a place to talk. This is an art. There will be a lot of awkward silence -- especially when you start. That's okay. Keep posting anyway.

Sometimes starting the conversation means being the one to reply to someone else's post. As a Facebook Page, you can interact and follow other Pages. This gives your brand quite a bit of visibility -- especially over time. This is Robert Nissenbaum's[15] strategy, and it works for him time and time again.

LinkedIn Company Pages operate much in the same way as Facebook Pages. People can follow Company Pages, but Company Pages cannot interact in the home feed. When someone does take the time to comment on a post, like their comment, respond to it. Otherwise, this is a missed opportunity you may never gain again.

Twitter and Instagram allow people and companies to interact with one another on a level playing field. For this reason, we see them as great opportunities for starting the conversation. Spend time each day commenting on other posts and replying to tweets. Don't just respond to comments you get. That's not proactive; it's reactive. Starting the conversation on social media is a combination of hospitality and outreach.

A successful conversation requires three things:

1. something of value and interest to each person,
2. proximity,
3. technique and etiquette, so a connection is made, and we can have future conversations.

---

[15] https://tacticalsocialmedia.org/

Building a Relationship

Just like relationships in real life (IRL), social media relationships – good ones – require effort. This may seem like hard work. You will only get out of your relationship, your project, your social media platform, what you put in. If you don't work at it, you will end up with an inferior product. What's the product? It's the relationship. So yes, it takes effort, but when you exercise empathy, it becomes second nature.

The Beginning of a Beautiful Relationship

We live with a constant flow of information via print, radio, TV, the internet, and between our family, friends, and colleagues. Our attention is always being joggled by another attempt to "start a conversation" about the best coffee brand, a place for dinner, the best route to the airport, or the latest political fallout.

Successful people and businesses know how to communicate. They connect with us even as we are bombarded with endless messages every day. We want to hear what they say, so we take the time to listen. We can, in our personal and working life, become effective communicators. This equips us to have valuable conversations with clients, colleagues, and our social media circles. **Without a real conversation, we make no connection.**

Developing skills and understanding the etiquette necessary for effective conversation is a critical part of learning every day.

Learning to communicate effectively is part of our socialization. Markets, relationships, brands – these all require good conversations to survive.

That we have something of value to communicate is just as important as **how we communicate**. We require the tools to continue the relationships and engagement of the people in the conversation. Those tools are questions. What do people want to know? How will it improve their life and yours? How can your business be helpful online?

Without a real conversation, we make no connection. Our communication becomes banter. Jibber jabber. Noise. It's meaningless and annoying, like a banner ad we might see competing for our attention on a website that we would never, ever, click on.

Conversations don't just happen like magic or well-programmed AI. The tools we need to engage aren't software and hardware; but strategy, empathy, and focus. Don't follow the siren song of automation; those conversations aren't real. They won't build affinity.

Affinity leads to loyalty; loyalty leads to sales.

Maintain Loyalty

Gaining loyalty is easy; maintaining it is not. Many retail shops offer loyalty programs; you know, from the baker's dozen to the buy 10, get $5 off the next round. Customers need more than that to keep loyalty. Meaning, you have to keep the deals you started with.

If the donut store we've been referencing suddenly stops selling apple fritters. Why! That's an abomination. That's the only thing you liked there. Or what if they moved 20 minutes across town? Now they're not on the way to work; no reason to stop there for a pink box of sugary heaven.

In the States right now, AT&T is pushing hard for their new campaign where new _and existing customers_[16] get the best deals on smartphones. You can't even watch a basketball game without hearing these commercials. Why did they make the change? Their website says,

> *"We're always listening to our customers. They've asked for more value, savings, and deals when it comes to their wireless needs. So, we're making it simple for them to get some of the best deals on smartphones we've ever offered."*

What's the catch? You have to be an existing customer who is "well-qualified." There's always a catch. Reasonable? You'll be the judge of that.

So, how can you effectively maintain loyalty? Listen to your existing customers. Include them on exclusive sneak peeks. Maybe your donut shop invites your customers (and they have

---

[16] https://about.att.com/story/2020/att_offers.html

to give their email to be invited) to a tasting. Existing customers may have the chance to vote for new options or have them a week ahead. What would this look like in your business?

Bridget gives existing customers 15% off new plans when they add to their existing monthly plans. She gives discounts for bulk prepayment of services. She keeps old rates. New customers get new rates. Old customers don't get screwed. That's how you keep and maintain loyalty with your existing customer base.

Tell People What You Do

Once we, as small business owners, get into the rhythm of being social, it's easy to forget to tell people what we do. It's important to strike a balance. No one wants to feel like a used car salesman (no offense), but we need to talk about our products and services. So, how do we strike that balance?

A content planner will generally help you strike a balance. Do you need a special planner? Maybe. It's whatever works for you. Bridget likes to use Google Sheet; Warren likes post-it notes. Kim Doyal has a content planner in the form of a notebook[17]. The point being, it's important to make a plan that works.

The best tool is the one you use.

---

[17] https://contentcreatorsplanner.com/product/content-marketing-planner-calendar/

How often should you post?

This is a question that is brought up often. The answer is this. You should post as often as you consistently can while responding to notifications promptly.

This might mean that you tweet once a day. That's fine. It's not going to give you growth, but it will keep you active on that channel.

The next question after how often you should post is how often you should post about yourself?

How often should you post about yourself?

Whether you're sharing on Facebook, posting on LinkedIn, or tweeting on Twitter, we're going to use the verb "post." A good rule of thumb is to post once to every two posts that promote other people. Meaning, you share (tweet or post) links to your website, videos, and any other promotional properties ⅓ of the time. This helps you stay focused on consistently telling people what you do while still being social.

Example Weekly Posting Schedule for Donut King About Themselves:

- Monday: Write a blog post about the most popular donuts that sold out this weekend.
- Tuesday: Share that blog post on Twitter

- Wednesday: Share an artful photo of your store when it's first opening in the early morning, telling people you wake up early to make their stomachs warm.

- Thursday: Write on your Facebook Page telling people the weekly specials since the weekend is coming up.

- Friday: Post an Instagram Story about the best times to show up before the most popular donuts sell out.

- Saturday: Tweet out a list of your specials. Use your local hashtag.

- Sunday: Everyone knows that Sundays are for coffee and donuts and snuggling with your favorite someone. Post a photo of coffee on Instagram. Make sure to use your local hashtag.

Now, that would be seven days of posting about yourself. So what would be the rest of the 21 posts that aren't all about Donut King?

We're glad you asked.

Example Weekly Posting Schedule for Donut King About The Industry:

- Monday: 1. Share a post from your local newspaper on your Facebook Page. 2.Tweet out a news article about the most popular donuts.

- Tuesday: 1. Share an article on LinkedIn about the behind-the-scenes business of donuts and on-the-go snacks. 2 Share a blog post from a popular donut maker machine on home recipes.

- Wednesday: 1 Instagram post of the yummy snack in your hand as you get the crowd on your side before the big weekly meeting begins. 2 Snapchat or TikTok posts?

- Thursday: 1. Write a local business review on their Google My Business listing. 2 shouts out to a partner business.

- Friday: 1. What interesting fact about donuts from around the world would be interesting for your audience? 2. Share a video you found on YouTube about the history of donuts.

- Saturday: 1. Post a tweet highlighting a local business. #ShopSmall 2. Do it again.

- Sunday: 1. Post a funny article about how people take their coffee on Facebook. 2. Ask people what their favorite donut was as a child.

Did you notice which social media platform was left off of this list? Instagram. Yep. It's against the terms of service to regram or repost. Instagram requires original content.

> "The short answer is that it's not okay to #regram under either the Instagram Terms of Use or Community Guidelines." (Stahle)

What should you post?

Ah-ha! We finally got to the $60,000 question. What should you share on social media? This is where creating a plan is important -- especially until you get used to posting regularly.

A good rule of thumb is to share content that inspires you, is local to you, and is about you. So, inspiration, local, you. You can do this!

What inspires you?

What inspired you this week? Was it the book you're reading or an article you read? Maybe it was a documentary or a conversation you had with a friend.

One of Bridget's favorite TED talks is Steven Johnson's "Where Good Ideas Come From.[18]" It is fascinating how he tells the story of the coffee houses to the satellites that allow us to find coffee houses. We both read his book Wonderland. So, what would you post?

Bridget posted a photo of a sculpture she saw at the Dallas Arboretum of children dancing with one of his quotes.

Bridget Willard @BridgetMWillard · Oct 18, 2019 · · ·
All great innovation comes from play.

"You'll find the future wherever people are having the most fun."
@StevenBJohnson bit.ly/2iljtnk

#Innovation

---

https://www.ted.com/talks/steven_johnson_where_good_ideas_come_from?language=en

Here's a screenshot of a tweet from Warren saying that he is excited to read a couple of new books, including the one from Steven Johnson.

What's local to you?

You may come across local information that is important to share. In the age of COVID, there's plenty of that. It could also be weather information, a business that is having a sale, or an oddity.

In this Tweet, Bridget ties in her local city with the Harvard Business Review article she's reading.

 Bridget Willard @BridgetMWillard · Feb 9   · · ·
San Antonio is hot!

@HarvardBiz shows that there is 400% growth for Fortune 500 Corporate Headquarters here.

#SATX

cc @VisitSanAntonio

In this tweet, Warren points out the irony of a sign that isn't local but ads that can be.

Warren Laine-Naida @WarrenLNaida · Feb 4

Today in class we taught a unit on target groups and retargeting in Google Ads with @joerggeissler

Ironically today an Ad for a Bavarian soccer team but here in Bremen 😂

#TargetGroups #Advertising

What about you?

Yes, you are encouraged to share posts promoting your content, business, and brand. Please do. So often, we don't know that people are taking clients, selling do-dads, or whatnot. We can't read your minds. We need to know, which means you need to post about it.

In this tweet, Rhonda Negard[19] shares one of her blog posts, a case study showing how she helped her client. Those are perfect pieces of content to share online.

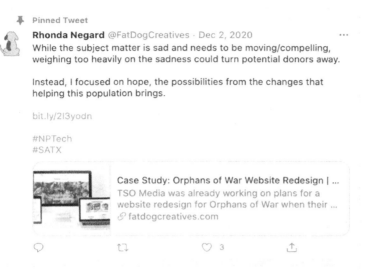

Posting doesn't have to be complicated. We make it complicated by being afraid of failing. Honestly, unless you're a hateful person who doesn't censor yourself, it's pretty hard to mess up online.

Jot down a few ideas. Play with your brand's voice. And have fun! The more you post, the more you'll find your voice. It takes time -- for everyone.

In this next post, Annabelle Deisler[20] shows both the product (Home Office by Corner Office[21]) and the attitude we all have with working at home right now.

---

[19] https://twitter.com/FatDogCreatives
[20] https://www.instagram.com/annabelledeisler/
[21] https://www.corneroffice.store/

annabelledeisler · Following   ...

annabelledeisler #HomeOffice n
stuff... I literally LIVE in these pants.
Get yours now on @_corner_office_
😎👖

3w

annabelledeisler #homeoffice
#homeofficedecor
#HomeOfficeIdeas
#homeofficedesign
#homeofficeday
#homeofficefurniture
#homeofficers
#homeofficeproblems
#homeofficeinspo
#homeofficeview
#homeofficevibes
#HomeOfficeTips

Liked by warrenlnaida and 91 others

JANUARY 18

Add a comment...

Social Media Checklist

Do you have the following?

- Roadmap of goals?

- Audience definition?

- Plan of action when something goes wrong?

- Social media guidelines and workflow for your team or yourself?

- Integration of your social media with your print and other campaigns?

- Do you have the time, people, and budget in place?

- Content creation plan?

- Measurement plan?

- Do you have partnerships and/or influencers in place?

- Up-To-Date Google My Business Listing?

- Other rating tools in place or audited including Yelp, Trip Advisor, Trust Pilot.

- Usernames that are consistent across social networks?

- Consistent header and profile images across social networks?

- Yoast SEO or Rank Math on your website to optimize how your website looks on social?

- (Have you audited your entire online presence?)

- Access to photography you are allowed to use online? (Your photos, Unsplash.com, or a subscription to a service)

Your First Social Media Steps

Baby steps. Perhaps you haven't taken your first steps on Social Media. Perhaps you have privately, but not for your business. It might seem scary, unnecessary, too much work. When Facebook came out in 2007, we were thinking, "Oh, this is cool." Never did we imagine it would be a business tool. Google+ has come and gone. MySpace is irrelevant. Even the much-touted virtual business world from twenty years ago, Second Life is gone. Platforms come and go, but what remains constant is our need to connect with people and tell them about ourselves and our product.

Finding the Right Type of Shoes

Think about the last time you went jogging. You wore your jogging shoes. To the mall, your walking shoes. To the forest, your hiking boots. Picking the right type of shoes for your activity is the same as picking the right type of social media platform for your marketing. You don't need to rush in and use every Social Media platform. Perhaps Facebook is enough, or Twitter or Instagram. Each platform is a tool, so decide what you want to do and which tool is the best for you.

Building community? Facebook. Sending news? Twitter. Are photos important to your business? Instagram. Serious corporate connectivity? Linkedin. Downloads and shareables? Pinterest. Online learning and media? YouTube.

You can begin with one tool and move to another as resources and need a permit. Baby steps.

Social Media's importance and our connected, mobile, instantaneous world changed how we market and communicate. It has enabled us to move from a monologue to a dialogue. We can immediately find out how customers like or dislike what we are doing. We can ask for feedback and get it immediately - and - we get this feedback from a real person. Social Media is measurable and specific dialogue.

Social Media is more than a post or a tweet. It is about relationships, involvement, engagement, honesty, reciprocity, respect, authenticity, motivation, interest, and influence. That's a pretty powerful set of tools!

The Proof of the Pudding is in the Eating

You don't know how something will work out until it's done. That's why testing in small batches is always best. Are we the only ones who fry off a small patty to taste before we fry off the entire batch for the team? Perhaps. With social media, it's a bit more difficult. Your post might go out and be shared by hundreds before you notice you spelled donuts 'donuts!

Our success on social media as a marketing tool is based on the concept of social proof. Social proof is the social currency we collect over time through our posts, shares, likes, and comments. It is not unique to social media; social capital has always existed. Our decisions have always been based on what others say and do. The Wisdom of the Crowd is a powerful thing, and we tend to rely on that to make our decisions.

At the top of the social proof, pecking orders are our family and friends. We listen to them the most. Then come experts in the field. Celebrities and influencers come next. That's a lot of people to listen to! We are also influenced in our decision-making by our political and religious beliefs. The brands we follow are also there, influencing our decisions. Together they make up the pudding we dig into to find the acceptance, or proof, of what we do.

Listen First, Talk Later

How can we find out what's being said? How can we get into the conversation? We listen. On social media, we listen just as we do at a party or a conference. Who is saying what? Who is the up-and-coming person? What is the next trend? Where should we place our bets? These questions predate social media but now come at us more frequently because of it.

Social media conversation rules are the same as in our off-line lives. Listen, ask questions, understand when not to speak. Don't just talk about yourself. Get people into the conversation. Make it about the bigger picture.

> *"That's a very good point. Hi, I'm Jaimie. Did I hear you say you were from Iowa? My friend Jessie is, too.*

Jessie, this is Alex. Alex also works in the business.
What were you saying about flour to me last week?"

Be the glue that binds people together on social media. Be a destination people want to come to. Be a conversation people want to join and share.

Storytelling

People connect and socialize best around a story. Storytelling is probably the oldest tradition we have. Stories are portable, translatable, and they can be changed by adding personalized details. Have you ever played the game where one person says something, and by the time it gets to the end of the room, the story is completely different? That needn't be a bad thing.

Stories convey not just a product -- they convey your business's traditions, values, and culture. As stories are shared so easily and rapidly, a great story is ideal for sharing social media. Finding a story that fits your product, brand, business, as well as who you are, is a worthwhile investment in your marketing.

Selling donuts? No, you are selling happiness.

Selling shoes? No, you are selling movement.

Selling meat? No, you are selling our mastery of fire.

Selling clothes? No, you are selling beauty.

Make your story about more than your product. Make your social media about more than you. Make it about what you offer to people.

Help! I'm a Really Poor Storyteller

Step 1: Crystal clear positioning. What exactly is it you do? Think big. Make it epic!
Step 2: Develop your concept. A story can be text, images, or a video.

Step 3: Adapt core message to the target group - each story needs to speak to someone.

Step 4: Find the theme of your story. Will this be a tear-jerker? Or a heroic quest?

Step 5: Write your script, find your music but keep it short! The story must be easily remembered. 30 seconds.

Step 6: Adapt your story to your communication channels. A video for YouTube, a question and answer for Facebook, an image for Instagram, an infographic for Pinterest, data for LinkedIn.

Wait. This Sounds Like Content Marketing!

Indeed! Content Marketing involves persuading customers with informative and relevant content instead of monologue advertising. Content Marketing's focus is offering added value while showing how our product will make the life of a customer better. Storytelling is a basic way to inspire using a takeaway!

Step 5 -- Paid Online Advertising

Free versus Paid Advertising

We've already talked about how you can improve your chances of being found with SEO, and you can also increase the likelihood of being found by using SEA -- or Search Engine Advertising. You will often hear SEA referred to as Pay Per Click or PPC.

We know what you're thinking,

> *"I don't have an advertising budget!"*

We're going to ask you to hold off on closing your mind -- just for now. Okay?

SEA includes paid measures for an improved brand presence within search engine results. Combined with organic marketing, paid ads appearing in a search engine, such as Google, can improve the likelihood of your website being found. Sound complicated? Here's the bottom line: pair your ad budget with your social media to improve findability. It's a win-win.

Here's an example. Our donut shop collects numerous links, improves its URL structure and landing pages (SEO). While improving technical SEO, the shop simultaneously books ads displayed on the search results page, at the top and the bottom (SEA).

When our donut shop publishes recipes on their website as blog posts, they use Content Marketing to be found. The SEA (the search engine ads we booked) informs us which terms users are searching for. Those keywords that we want to be associated with us can also be included in our blogging topics!

Example: We see in our ad report that people are searching for "order donuts online." This search is activating the ads we have booked. We can use this search string and include it in our blog post. Perhaps we write about the difference between donuts that are ordered online and those bought in the shop. When people search for "order donuts online," they may see our ad AND our blog post. We can even save some money and deactivate that ad now that we have another way for people to see us in the search results. See how that works?

It's a win-win for the donut shop since they essentially gain more of the real estate in a search. This is also why ensuring your Google My Business Listing is filled out.

Don't be discouraged. You are not out of the race if you don't buy ads! 70% of people indeed click on organic search results, and 30% are likely to click on ads. Paid links and other media are only a small part of your potential marketing toolbox. This is why we took so much time in Steps 3 and 4. Getting your SEO and social media tightened up is about 80% of the work.

> *"When you build brand equity elsewhere, Google and Facebook become better channels." Rand Fishkin of Spark Toro*[22]

---

[22] https://youtu.be/XAK7WSxGtYU

What Types of Marketing Media Are Available to Your Business?

Not everyone has a budget to pay for ads or the time to monitor them. Sometimes Online Marketing can be overwhelming. However, advertising, or Paid Media, is just one of the tools in your marketing Swiss Army Knife. Three types of Media are also available to you: Owned Media, Shared Media, and Earned Media. Together, these three are a powerful way to market your business. Do you have a website (owned media), a social media account (shared media), and happy customers (earned media)? Then you already have the Three Musketeers of Marketing!

Owned Media: Your Website, Newsletter, Shop

Simply stated, owned media is content you own. You own your website. You own your newsletter. You own your eCommerce shop -- ideally, of course. You could have your website on proprietary software that you can't easily export but stick with us.

You have complete control over this type of Owned Media. However, you must supervise and control the process from start to finish yourself or hire an agency to manage it for you.

The advantages of owned media are portability, control over the content, control over timing, "free" publishing, and freedom of design.

Advantages Of Owned Media:

- Complete control over content and timing as well as duration;
- Free publishing; and,
- placement that can be guaranteed and designed.

Earned and Shared Media: Reviews, Ratings, Social Media, Press

Earned media is the best! Why? You have to work hard for Earned Media and, if you get it, you can pat yourself on the back for a job well done. Earned Media is all of the content that third parties publish about you and your company. This content is created and published by consumers, bloggers, and journalists without being commissioned by the company.

Advantages of Earned and Shared Media:

- Increased credibility;
- free publication;
- greater reach; and,
- more intensive brand perception.

Paid Media: Google Ads, Affiliate Ads, Social Media Ads, Print Ads, Radio or TV Ads

Paid Media is any kind of paid advertising on the web. This includes any marketing or advertising campaigns that you have to pay for.

Advantages of Paid Media:

- Control over message content and form, as well as duration and budget;
- increase reach in a short time;
- Generate targeted traffic for a specific goal; and,
- Improve the performance of owned media.

Google Ads

How Do Google Paid Ads Work?

With Google Ads, you target potential customers who search for businesses like yours in Google Search or on Google Maps. You only pay for results, such as clicks that take users to your website or call your business.

Paid ads work on the principle of "See, Think, Do, Care" or "Attention, Interest, Desire, and Action." This has been a basic marketing principle for many years -- before the existence of the internet.

Google offers two different types of paid ads. First, those ads we see when we search for something. These are text and shopping ads that appear within the organic search results when we search for products and services. The second types are banner or video ads that appear on websites or in YouTube videos. These are called display ads and appear not while we are looking for something but because they are probably of interest because of other websites we have visited or products we have viewed.

Ideally, we would like to have visitors click on our ads and then make a purchase; but this doesn't always happen. Don't worry; Google ads can be used for much more than selling things.

What are the Pros and Cons of Google Paid Ads?

Targeting: advertisers can address their customers specifically. In doing so, you set criteria from age to place and time to gender yourself. With skill, you can then out-compete even your larger competitors.

Fast and flexible: You can pause, change, adjust or edit ads and budgets as needed. Unlike print or radio advertising, this allows you to react quickly to changes. Being agile is important for small business marketing.

Cost control: Even with a small budget, you can target a campaign. You only pay when an action (such as clicking on an ad) has taken place. The previously-set budget is not exceeded. Does success come? You can adjust the budget up or down at any time.

Measurability: You can use the data on click-through rates (CTR) and costs to measure a campaign's effectiveness. If applicable, this also allows you to determine the cost-effectiveness of your ad spend. Were your sales at the level you expected for the ad budget?

Reduced wastage: By defining keywords, an ad is only shown when someone searches for the term in question. Ads are, therefore, delivered specifically to potential customers.

Just in time: Someone wants to order donuts, and you are a donut delivery service? Perfect! Place an ad in the right place at the right time. With ad extensions, customers can also reach you directly by phone. With people searching on their mobile devices, this is perfect.

Placing Google ads can bring you a decisive advantage. However, there are some other considerations to keep in mind as well. You need the good news and the bad news.

Time-consuming training: Anyone who thinks that an advertising campaign via Google ads can be set up quickly is right. A car can also be built quickly, but will it be any good? Google offers numerous functions and stumbling blocks that inexperienced users quickly get hung up on. It's pretty easy to blow $3,000 if you don't know what you're doing. Ask us. We have case studies.

Missing the mark: If you start advertising without the proper strategy and planning, you could quickly burn through a lot of money without achieving your company's goal. Again, it's better to know this before you start.

Not the right product: Google ads might not be the pay-per-click tool best suited for your company. Explore all your options. Consider social media ads and other platforms, as well as Google Ads.

Creating Google Ads Step by Step

Creating Google ads utilizes some of the same steps we took to create your SEO plan. Do you not yet have a Google Ads account? You can set one up easily[23] right now.

1. Define the goals and positioning of your business

2. Understand your customers/users

3. Define the goals of your advertising campaign

4. Adapt your advertising campaign to your landing page

5. Adapt your ads to keywords Google provides that match your landing page

6. Develop different variations of your ads

7. Controlling (daily, measuring) of your campaign

8. Use keyword tools to optimize[24] your AdWords campaign

---

[23] https://ads.google.com
[24] https://support.google.com/google-ads/answer/6167110

Google Ads Case Study

Headline: Using Google Ads for Lead Generation and Search Engine Optimisation

Client: Rachel Fowler Interiors[25]

Rachel is a commercial and residential interior designer with offices in Hamburg, Germany, and Berkshire, UK. Her focus is sustainable, animal-friendly interior design.

The Goal: Generating Visibility and Clients

Lead generation and brand awareness are very competitive environments. Also, operating an English-speaking business in a German city makes running Google Ads and Google My Business challenges. Sustainable design is an important issue in both the UK and Germany and does add value to our search terms and blog content marketing.

Interior Design is a highly competitive market. Added to that was the fact that people were spending a lot more time at home because of the lockdowns that were in place in Europe in 2020 and 2021. The winter months are traditionally when people think about renovations and interior changes to be realized in the upcoming summer months. Rachel was interested in being present in Google search results and becoming more active on social media. The goal was to become a part of the conversation about sustainable interior design.

---

[25] https://rachelfowlerinteriors.com/

With the heavy competition in the industry, being yet another voice in the crowd was not enough. Rachel's message addresses an issue over-and-above simply repapering a room and adding a kitchen island. It needed to be about long-term change and becoming a partner in that change.

How We Combined Google Ads with SEO and Social Media:

For the two quarters from Q4 2020 and Q1 2021, Rachel was enabled in two ways. First, via Social Media connections and Q&As. These were bolstered with Content Marketing via her blog posts. At the beginning of our work together, Rachel's goal was to get into a conversation with potential clients, suppliers, and market makers. By the end of the second quarter, she was "overwhelmingly busy" and "very happy" with the transformation that had occurred on social media. She was in conversations with people, and her posts were being shared by others. Connecting and being a part of the conversation is one important way to connect with potential clients while adding value to her website blog posts.

Secondly, revamping Rachel's Google My Business listing meant not just her company name was being found, but also blog posts, products. More importantly, relevant search terms were being easily matched with her business. We added Google Ads to understand the search terms people were using when searching for interior designers and generate possible leads. These ads brought Rachel into contact with suppliers and clients. For a $1/day budget, Google Ads generated more than

280,000 impressions and almost 300 clicks. Two client leads made contact with Rachel. The ads' entire spend was 85 dollars, while a client's value to Rachel is tens of thousands of dollars.

The Social Media and Blog spend was zero, as was the Google My Business spend. Both of these things Rachel executed herself.

Step 6 -- Getting Permission: Email Marketing

When you think about email marketing, do you think of the junk ads you get every time you open up your email client? Do you think of the email that your high school friend sends you now that she's selling the best yoga pants that ever existed? One is sort of annoying; the other is annoying. (Okay. They are the best yoga pants, but you get it.)

Guess what? Email marketing works.

> *"A lot of businesses have the free opt-in offer, but then they don't follow up with those people. The best way is with a drip-email campaign." Amy Hall (WPwatercooler Network)*

Why Engage in Email Marketing?

Traditional email marketing doesn't mean dumping all of your contacts into an email you compose on AOL. (Wait, you're not still using America Online or Hotmail, are you?) Be that as it may, email marketing works. Why? Because people opted in. They chose to be part of your list. They want to hear from you.

When properly planned and executed, email marketing builds upon the relationships you started, develops your brand (in the customer's eyes), builds your credibility, and more! When people like you, they like your brand. That emotional connection or feeling toward you is called affinity.

Affinity leads to loyalty, and loyalty leads to sales. Every day of the week.

Of all the marketing tactics we have in our tool belts, email marketing is the most efficient and budget-conscious method. So why not try it?

Build Affinity with Email Marketing

Engaging with your audience (interested people from a landing page or chamber of commerce) regularly is a sure way to build affinity. As long as the content of your emails is easy-to-read, short, and useful, they'll keep opening them.

Throughout your email relationship, you develop your unique brand in their eyes. We call this brand awareness. What we want is for them to think of a Kleenex when they want a tissue, an Uber when they need a ride, and Apple when they need a computer. Essentially, you provide enough value that your audience likes you and is very aware of you (they'll most likely start referring you to their friends at this point). Affinity's BFF is brand awareness. They go hand-in-hand.

Build Loyalty with Email Marketing

After purchase, it's important to continue the relationship with your customer. We've all heard it said that it is much more difficult to gain a new customer than to keep one. So let's keep our customers.

Creating a nurture campaign post-purchase is a great way to build a strong customer relationship. Firstly, you'll want to thank your customer for the purchase. Secondly, you'll want to educate them on best practices while using your product continuously. You may also want to suggest a companion product.

If your customers purchase a service from you, the same applies. So if they hired you to design their home, perhaps they will need your remodeling services. Also, what's the best style of furniture for their new massive home with 30-foot ceilings? Mid-century modern? Probably not. The scale is off.

As you nurture that customer relationship, you bring them into the delight phase of the relationship.

Build Sales with Email Marketing

Getting one sale is easy. How about repeated business or referrals? Loyalty leads to sales. It can be said that loyalty can lead to more sales. As you continue your outreach campaigns, landing pages to address different audiences, you will see that your email marketing truly builds your credibility as a business.

You're providing weekly or monthly value to the best place you can be invited: a user's mailbox. You're the expert sharing these tips with them. It feels personal, exclusive. Your audience will, inevitably, tell their friends and family about your service. How simple is it for a customer to forward an email?

Happy clients, who refer more work to you, can also be rewarded. Whether it's a discount code or coupon, a surprise addition to their next order a la Zappos, or a gift card, rewarding loyal clients and customers will bring them back to affinity and reinforce their loyalty.

Loyalty can't just be gained; it has to be maintained as well.

Why Do You Need Permission to Email?

There are two aspects to marketing, which every small business already knows, so we will not spend too much time telling you what you already know. There is talking at people and talking with people. Which gets you better results? Right, talking with people.

To talk with people, we need permission. We need to be invited into the conversation, or in the case of door-to-door sales, invited into the home. When we are permitted to enter, we need to be respectful -- or we won't be invited again.

This basic premise is at the heart of email marketing. It is not enough to understand what you are legally *allowed* to do -- to be respectful of a person's private sphere (email, social media, chat messenger, telephone) -- you need to know what you should *not* do.

In the USA, you have the Federal CAN-SPAM Act as well as state regulations. In Europe, you have GDPR data laws. These regulate what we can and cannot do to contact people and use their personal data; this includes sending them emails. Yes, you can be subject to large fines for every instance of non-compliance. More than this, if your email marketing is spam, then how are you gaining trust? You're not. That's even more detrimental to your marketing efforts.

Trust and permission go hand-in-hand. If you want to be successful in email marketing, you need to be a good people person. You need to know when not to cross the line.

What We Mean By Permission

Only email people who have given you their email address for that purpose. Did they give you their email address for marketing purposes? Or did they give it to you as a part of their warranty agreement? Just because you have their email doesn't mean you have permission.

Know When to Email

Would you ask someone to marry you if you only just met? Possibly. How romantic! Email is not romantic. There are five stages to your relationship with your clients, and email comes at the end, not the beginning.

1. "Getting to know you, getting to know all about you." Lead generation. Website visits and search engine optimization. Who are your visitors, and what do they want? Are you the right match? Intent!

2. Connecting that intent with ads. Putting your money where your mouth is. Is there a spark? A second date? Did they click on your search ad?

3. Display ads are where retargeting steps up to bat. The first connection was great, now will you meet my parents? Did a visit to your website generate a sale or at least a newsletter registration?

4. Permission level 1 -- Social Media -- let's talk. Share pictures and get to know each other on a more personal level. Your relationship is now in public.

5. Finally - Step 5 - the ultimate permission. Yes, I do! You have been permitted to email them. Don't mess it up. One wrong email at the wrong time and you're back to Step 1, drinking martinis at the Hilton and checking your hair in the sugar bowl -- alone.

Respect

Sometimes the relationship just doesn't work. That can happen. The spark isn't there like it used to be. You need to know when to let go. You must allow people to unsubscribe. We know, big lists. Everyone wants vanity metrics. And companies love to know how many people are on your lists. Podcasts live and die by their email lists

"Your message must include a clear and conspicuous explanation of how the recipient can opt-out of getting an email from you in the future." Federal Trade Commission CAN-SPAM Act[26]

Instead of hiding your unsubscribe options, make it another place to show your personality. I made my email footer font big on purpose. Jason Resnick[27] uses emoji in his.

---

[26] https://www.ftc.gov/tips-advice/business-center/guidance/can-spam-act-compliance-guide-business

[27] https://rezzz.com/

So, about this email.

I definitely don't want to bug you. Want to change how you receive these emails?

You can update your preferences **or** unsubscribe from this list.

I won't be too bummed. I get it. Though, you'll **miss out on my weekly insight**, tools I find, and basically a friend.

Copyright © 2021 Bridget Willard, LLC, All rights reserved.
You are receiving this email because you have purchased a download, contacted me for a quote, signed up for a specific drip, or are a current or past client.

Our mailing address is:
Bridget Willard, LLC

Jason Reznick's email footer is cute and shows personality.

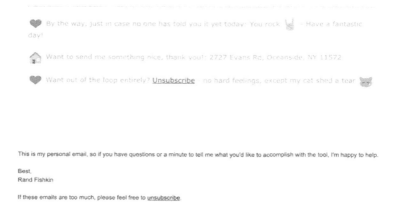

Rand Fishkin's[28] **email footer is simple and reads well.**

---

[28] https://sparktoro.com/

What's the Advantage of a Small List?

You don't have a busload of friends, but those you do remember your birthday and anniversary every year? That sounds like a good group of people to have around. A bird in the hand is worth two that are not.

A small list doesn't get subscribers to your podcast, but the flip side is intimacy. Email marketing brings intimacy back to businesses -- especially in COIVID times. We long to hear from someone on the other side. We want them to read our message in the bottle. We want to relate with them and how they're doing business during the pandemic.

You don't need a big list. You need the right list. Your target audience is the only one you need.

Make Lists

Everyone makes lists. We make them all the time. Groceries, ToDos, shows to watch, books to read, places to visit. Email lists are just as useful. Think about why you want to email someone, and there you have a list. Be TRUE to these lists. Remember, no one likes getting an email offer for a free set of cookware when all they signed up for was your monthly newsletter about hair care.

What sort of Emails Can I Send?

Welcome emails:	Use this wisely; it may be the start of a beautiful relationship.
Confirmation emails:	This is an automatic double opt-in email that uses receive when they sign up for your newsletter or other offers.
Seasonal emails:	Use wisely with seasonal greetings, offers, advice. This is still a marketing email.
Post-Purchase Drip emails:	How was the product? How was the experience? Ask questions.
Connect-Via-Social emails:	Use subtly and wisely. Do you have a new channel?
Cart Abandonment emails:	Use wisely; people aren't stupid. They didn't forget to click buy! They may be gaming your system.
Re-Engagement emails:	Use wisely; people may have forgotten you, but they may also have moved on.
Newsletter emails:	These people only get your newsletters.

Birthday emails:	These people only get birthday greetings and a nice rebate gift.
Marketing offer emails:	These people you can send your product offers -- within reason. How often? How often do YOU like receiving these types of emails?
Support emails:	These people should only be used if an issue exists that affects support and maintenance. It is not a sales list.

What lists can you think of that would be relevant to your business?

I don't want so many lists.

You don't need to. Email clients enable you to have one email list and to segment your master list into "newsletter only," "support only," "marketing only," "cookware," "cat and dog care," "local customers," or "regional customers." However, your business needs to segment your audience; it is possible in any email marketing client.

Why Do You Need an Email Client?

No, you can't just email from your Gmail account. Why? You can be marked as spam for one thing. Also, it's not professional. You have no reporting, and people have no way to opt-out or unsubscribe. So, why do you need a CMS for your website? Why do you need Instagram? Why do you need a hosting provider for your website? Why do you need a tax advisor? You can't do everything yourself. You need to spend your time where it matters -- in front of the client.

An email client saves time, guides you through the process, saves you from making mistakes, watches out for the legal cans and cannots, saves your mailing list for you, generates reports on openings and clicks, and more. Bonus? For the most part, they can be free.

We both prefer Mailchimp[29]. Do you have less than 2000 contacts? Then this platform is FREE. Thirteen million businesses use Mailchimp, and as they say, they were a small business once, too. Mailchimp is "everything we wish we had way back when to help you do your thing today."

CleverReach, SendinBlue, ConstantContact, and ActiveCampaign all allow you to create a drip or nurture campaign. Drip campaigns allow you to educate your subscriber after purchasing a product or subscribing to a list. It's automated, and the subscriber starts with the welcome email and receives the series based upon when they signed up. Nurture campaigns are also automated, and part of your sales process and is triggered by a consumer's behavior on your

---

[29] https://mailchimp.com/

website. Potato PoTAHto? Maybe. Either way, drip and nurture campaigns are not your weekly newsletter.

How do we get started with Email Marketing?

Step 1: Set your goals

Step 2: Build your email list

Step 3: Choose the type of campaigns you want to send out

Step 4: Create your first campaign

Step 5: Measure your results

Things to Remember

- Think retention, not just acquisition
- Be realistic
- Think frequency
- Test whatever you can
- Measure conversion, not just clicks
- Drip email Campaign
- Key benefits of drip email campaigns:
- Precise segmentation leads to more sales
- More engagement with less effort
- Continuous conversation to stay in mind

Next Steps -- Email Marketing Assignments

- Get out a paper and pen (or Google Docs) and write down the categories your customers fall into. A contractor would have Real Estate Professionals, Subcontractors, Clients, and Presales. (10 min)

- Write a welcome email to each of those audiences. Imagine they are sitting in your office, and they decided to subscribe to your email list. Be professional yet friendly. Include their name; let's go with "Bob." Express gratitude. (30 min)

- Choose an email marketing client. Mailchimp, Active Campaign and Constant Contact are the top email marketing clients. It won't be free, but it is a low-cost SaaS (Subscription as a Service). (20 min)

- If this step kind of freaks you out, you can always hire an email marketing specialist. They will ask you for the first three steps, so now you're ready. Create the tags or segments for each of those audiences.

- Upload a CSV for each of the email audiences. Be sure you have permission from them to email you. This is important for compliance with the CAN-SPAM Act.[30]

---

[30] https://www.ftc.gov/tips-advice/business-center/guidance/can-spam-act-compliance-guide-business

- Choose a simple email template (one photo max) for each one of your welcome messages. Copy/paste your text in the body of the email.

- Send out a test email. Ensure the *|FNAME|*[31] merge tag works.

- Follow the instructions for your email marketing client to schedule the send.

- At this point, you'll have to decide if you want an automated nurture campaign or send one manually every month. You'll also need to decide upon the frequency. It does depend upon your business and whether or not it has seasonality.

---

[31] This is the merge tag Mailchimmp uses for First Name.

Step 7 -- Measurement: Analytics and Tracking

Measure for Success - Analytics and Co

So far, your business has been doing everything right! You have a busy website, your social media is popular, and your online ads and email marketing bring in sales. Yay! How do you measure and evaluate all of this activity? And, what should you measure?

You have probably heard of Google, Adobe, or Matomo (formerly Piwik) analytics. In addition to the statistics available in your server log files, online advertising, social media, and email provider are two of the larger of the many analytics tools on the market. These tools allow you to analyze your website visitors and track their behavior.

Google Analytics presents statistics about a group of users of a website or app. Data is collected on the length of stay, the browser used, operating system, device, language setting, screen resolution, and user actions on the website. Those are the basics. You can always dig deeper, but you have more important things to do.

Tracking identifies individual user paths and their usage behavior. This allows the user to be shown individual advertising, logged-in user, or retargeting banner ad. Prices can even be customized depending on their geographic location. Individual identification in tracking allows personality profiles and behavior patterns to be formed.

Simply put, web analytics and tracking is the presentation of the data you collect on your website. It's the analysis. For your business, this data is exceedingly valuable.

How Do Analytics and Tracking Help My Business?

There is the "Aha moment" when we stand back and ask questions in everything we do. How did that work? Are we doing the right thing? Analytics and Tracking allow us to capture the impact of what we are doing on our website, social media, and advertising. It gives us the chance to measure our success or failure so that we can optimize our efforts.

What you can do with analytics and tracking:

- Measure your online traffic
- Optimize and track your marketing campaigns
- Track the success of your ads
- Learn about your audience
- Monitor the competition
- Optimize your website

- Optimize your Conversion Rate Optimisation (CRO)
- Track your business goals
- Develop new marketing ideas

What Should I Measure?

Most small businesses have two categories they measure: Marketing and Sales. You should make a distinction between evaluating your permanent performance in these areas and measuring to identify any weak points in your online shop, website, or other online marketing.

Marketing Analytics tracks your customer acquisition. Where do people come from?

Product Analytics track their engagement. What do people do, and why do they come and go from my website/online shop?

How Do I Measure?

Your business has many goals -- reduced business expenses, increased productivity, increased market share, increased community outreach, to name but a few. How close you are to realizing these goals can be seen via Key Performance Indicators (KPIs). KPIs can be viewed using the many Metrics available in your Analytics Dashboard.

Your goals need to be SMART (Specific, Measurable, Achievable, Reasonable, and Timely). For each goal, a Key

Performance Indicator (KPI) should be set as a measurement of your success.

Business Goal: Increased Market Share by 10%

> S: Increase Market Share in Old Town by 10% by the end of Q2 2021

> M: Measured by the number of products sold in Old Town compared with 2020

> A: We can achieve this goal with the new Sales hire we made

> R:10% is a reasonable lift year over year

> T: By the end of Q2 2021 (June 30, 2021)

KPI: Increased sales, especially in Old Town, where sales are traditionally low

Metrics: Amount of products sold, Amount sold in Old Town compared with 2020, Increased email newsletters to addresses in Old Town

Aren't Metrics also KPIs?

Every KPI is a Metric, but not every Metric is a KPI. Read that one again. (Marketers and our acronyms, right?) An important part of defining your business goals is the ability to measure them. "More sales" is too generic. Everyone wants more sales.

Think of Metrics like a football team. Every single person on the team is a player. But within the team, there is a smaller group that is solely tasked with stopping the ball, called the goalkeepers. There are also other players on the team -- defenders, centers, wingers. None of them, however, is a goalkeeper.

It's the same with KPIs and metrics. There are many metrics out there: Clicks, percentage of new sales, subscription revenue, visitors, etc., not all of them will be KPIs.

KPIs are the most important metrics you have -- the ones that underscore your key business goals.

Isn't all Measurement the Same?

Goodwill is difficult to measure in the monthly profit and loss statement. In the same way, some of your analytical measurements will be difficult to put your finger on. But don't be discouraged. "How many?" and "Why?" are the two types of numbers that interest every small business.

Qualitative analysis refers less to the data itself, being more focused on the question of How and Why they occurred. How delighted are our visitors with our new website? How do they feel?

Quantitative analysis is based on data and numbers regarding the visitors of a website, bounce rates, and other key numbers. How much product did we sell? Show me the money!

Both concepts are important to our bottom line. In contrast to the Quantitative success of our advertising (how many clicks or sales we achieved), the Qualitative success of our advertising does not focus on profit and sales but the impact of our advertising on our brand and our positioning. Traditionally this was known as "Good Will."

Set up a Google Analytics account here:

https://analytics.google.com/analytics/web

Set up a Matomo (Piwik) account here:

https://matomo.org

☐

Step 8 -- Playing Fair: Internet Rules and the Law

Internet Law - What I Need to Know

Some numerous principles and guidelines regulate your website and online shop. Some are ethical considerations, and some are legal requirements set out by local and federal law.

What's the difference, you ask? **Ethics** are standards and maxims of lifestyle derived from responsibility toward others. **Laws** are a set of norms of human behavior established by the state's legal system. Added to this is **Digital Ethics,** including personal privacy and data protection which are a hybrid mixture.

At the heart of this is the idea of a contract – an obligation between two parties. Understood in any contract is an expectation of trust. When people use your website, they do so voluntarily. Therefore, your diligence in making your website compliant with the law and expected ethical considerations can mean won or lost loyalty from your customers.

Why is Internet Law Important?

Online business, or the purchasing and selling items over the web, is slowly replacing the brick-and-mortar store. An online business has lower overhead and can, therefore, generate larger profits. The temptation to cut a few corners is great!

Internet laws and regulations are in place to help us combat spam, curb illegal online activities, protect minors, inhibit online fraud, and protect us against data theft and abuse.

Some laws differ from country to country and jurisdiction to jurisdiction. Ask for advice from a lawyer specializing in internet law for your country. Keeping in mind the ever-changing advances in online innovation and tools, internet law is a work in progress; therefore, when in doubt, don't do it!

http://library.law.columbia.edu/guides/International_Internet_Law

Let's first look at the ethics and fair play important to you as an online player.

Our Digital Rights and Freedoms

Digital rights are simply our human rights, but online. They are extensions of the equal and inalienable rights laid out in the United Nations' Universal Declaration of Human Rights[32].

---

[32] http://www.un.org/en/universal-declaration-human-rights/index.html

Some of our digital rights include:

- The right to intellectual property (e.g., "You can't use my picture on your site without my permission")

- The right to privacy (e.g., "Don't let the government co-opt encryption")

- The right to intellectual freedom ("Information wants to be free")

- The right to bandwidth ("Don't spam the net because it eats up resources that others need")

Wait. Isn't the Internet Free?

If we are talking about copyright law, the internet is no different than any other medium. The difference we see is that the internet is mostly "free to access" and reaches billions of people 24/7. That may give us the feeling that whatever we see is free for the taking. Just because the material on the internet is publicly accessible does not mean it belongs to everyone. It almost always does not.

Every country has its copyright laws, but you can assume if you didn't create it (video, photo, graphic, song, words, a pdf), it probably belongs to someone else.

Copyright References

- USA[33]

---

[33] https://www.copyright.gov/title17/92chap1.html

- [Canada](34)
- [UK](35)

Copyright on Creation

A copyright holder needn't inform us that content is copyrighted with a copyright notice. In the US, the 1976 Copyright Act states: "All content is copyright protected upon creation."

Be aware! If something is not protected by copyright law, it might be protected by trademark law. Some material is public domain and can be used without permission. Works dedicated to the public or works created before 1923. You should check your national copyright and trademark laws to be safe.

Get any permission in writing. If you are using the material you have purchased the rights to, be sure you can use it how you plan to. Certain royalty-free images still require a link to their owner. Certain images and music may not be used to sell things. Certain images you have purchased the license for may only be used for a specific period or may not be used on social media. Always read the license agreement.

But, what about the concept of Fair Use?

---

[34] https://www.ic.gc.ca/eic/site/cipointernet-internetopic.nsf/eng/h_wr02281.html
[35] https://en.wikipedia.org/wiki/Copyright_law_of_the_United_Kingdom

Fair Use

Chances are, you already know that "fair use" is a doctrine. This concept was incorporated into law in the Copyright Act that allows people to reproduce some or all parts of copyright-protected works without infringing on the exclusive rights the Act gives to authors.

The relevant statutory provision (17 U.S.C. § 107) describes four factors to consider when determining whether a particular use of a work is "fair:" the purpose and character of the use; the nature of the copyrighted work; the amount and substantiality of the portion used concerning the work as a whole; and the effect of the use on the potential market for, or value of, the original work.

In general, "fair use" tends to allow us to copyrighted material only for a "limited" and "transformative" purpose. For example, we may use portions of copyrighted works to comment on, criticize, or parody them. For these purposes, we do not need permission from the copyright holder. Basically, "fair use" defends us against infringement.

Why is Fair Use important?

The internet allows us to share media immediately and to many people with a touch of our finger. It was previously impossible or very difficult to copy and share images, videos, audio, and text.

Sharing digital media is different in three important ways:

1. We are active agents in the process of creating the meaning of media

2. We adopt, modify, manipulate and reform ways of understanding that media

3. We reflexively create our particular versions of that media

When we share and modify media and its meaning, we cross the Fair Use[36] line and enter Copyright and others' rights to their Intellectual Property.

Internet Regulations that Affect your Small Business Website and Online Shop

Some laws and regulations govern how your business operates that also impact your website - and as a small business, you probably already know about them. These include:

- Copyright, Trademarks, Patents

---

[36] https://en.wikipedia.org/wiki/Fair_use

- Terms and Conditions

- Sales, Shipping, Taxes

- Data Protection

What about your website? What regulatory considerations should you know about?

Your Website

- Is your website accessible to all users, including the disabled?

- Does it contain an imprint of ownership and authorship?

- Data protection information is laid out, including cookie information?

- Opt-out of cookies used by your website is available?

- Information on dispute resolution with a link to the responsible agency?

- Disclaimer of liability and copyright information visible?

Your Advertising

- Is your online advertising recognizable as such?

- Is the person on whose behalf advertising is made identifiable?

- Are promotional offers such as discounts, premiums, and gifts recognizable as such, the conditions for their use easily accessible and identifiable as such?

- Our contests or sweepstakes of a promotional nature also clearly identifiable as such, and the conditions for participation readily accessible as well as clearly and unambiguously stated?

Your Social Media

There are no clearly defined international laws about Social Media, but defamation of character, stalking, intellectual property theft, and copyright protection are enforced internationally. Also, each social media platform has its Community Standards to which we need to adhere.

Your company should also have standards about how Social Media is used, and most importantly, guidelines for when the conversation becomes unpleasant. An unhappy customer often uses Social Media to attack a company with whom they have had a bad experience. What do you do? What can you do?

A Social Media Policy is helpful to guide you through any entanglements quickly. This policy protects your employees, protects your brand, and reduces legal liability. There are many templates and examples available. We like the one you can download from Hootsuite[37].

- Define your team's roles
- Establish security protocols
- Make a plan of action for a security or PR crisis

---

[37] https://blog.hootsuite.com/social-media-policy-for-employees

- Guide how employees behave on their social media

- Encourage employees to take part in conversations around your brand

Your Online Shop

Online shops and eCommerce laws are important if we maintain standardized and trustworthy online transactions not just locally but across borders. Transactions should be straightforward and transparent, whether at your store or online. Any mistrust or lack of clarity could be extremely damaging to your business.

Note: You should inform yourself about any local, state, provincial, territorial, or federal laws that govern the processes of your online shop as well as the specific products or services that you sell.

General requirements of an online shop include:

- Provider identification

- Supplier identification

- Data protection declaration

- Privacy policy and imprint

- Data protection consent verifiably obtained (DoubleOpt-In) and logged

- Cookie notice (if required) integrated in a legally correct way (active Consent to non-mandatory cookies, revocation option, etc.)

- Data security ensured (SSL encryption for transmission of payment data)

- Information requirements for online dispute resolution (clickable link to the OSPlattform)

- Product description, both on the product page and on the order page

- Product images and other images/texts that are compliant

- Price information complete and correct

- Shipping costs and additional costs complete and correct

- Shipping costs linked before initiating the order process

- Payment options and delivery restrictions visible before the order process

- Delivery dates cleared stated

- Order process transparency (presentation of individual steps, correction options, available languages)

- Button solution - clear and understandable order summary, highlighted mandatory information, and correct button labeling

- Right of withdrawal linked on the order page

- Cancellation policy and sample cancellation policy

- General terms and conditions

- Conclusion of contract correct and transparent

- E-mail double opt-in and confirmation sent immediately after receipt of order

- Delivery of the goods with legal information on a durable data carrier

Does Everyone Do This? What are Some Common Hiccups?

- Incorrect or incomplete information in the imprint

- Incorrect or incomplete price information

- Incorrect or incomplete information on the consumer's right of return

- Inadmissible clauses in general terms and conditions

Legal requirements apply to all websites, regardless of their size, function, or target group. It doesn't matter who created your website or where it is registered. This is because you, as the operator/owner of the website, are liable for any defects or violations. Even existing websites should be improved accordingly if they do not (yet) meet requirements.

GDPR. GDPR Everywhere.

On May 27, 2019, the European GDPR/DSGVO took full effect, and our websites will never be the same. The law itself came into effect in 2016, but we were given a two-year grace period to bring our websites up to standard. For many people, the law came from nowhere, and compliance was left to the last minute – which was sort of like leaving a homework assignment from tenth grade until the bus ride into school the morning you are going to graduate from high school.

Social media went sort of berserk. According to hashtagify.me #DSGVO (the German form) was ninth in the top ten hashtags used in May 2019, almost doubling in popularity between March and June. However, in English, #GDPR was not nearly popular enough to make the top ten -- which might say something about Germany's love for rules.

Amidst the stress, many of us were thankful for the moments of brevity. We should all be thankful the tracking data websites all use called a cookie, for instance. Something we owe Lou Montulli, who coined the phrase "cookie" while working at Netscape.15 Thanks, Lou!

Among the good times were also frowny moments as we saw many overpriced and unnecessary offers of assistance to small businesses from unscrupulous agencies. This was not a time to prey on people who needed realistic and sensible advice rather than hundreds of euros in overbilling. Thanks go out to the many free checks and offer available by good companies and good consultants.

When we talk about personal data protection, we were probably still thinking about email, websites, and perhaps personal assistants like Alexa or Siri. Very soon, however, we may need to be thinking of protection in other terms. The Internet of Things (IoT) will mean not only refrigerators, coffee machines, and cars, but also clothing will be tracking our habits and sending our personal information back to the mothership.

The Silver Lining

In all, "GDPR-geddon" was an opportunity. We kept our websites up-to-date and compliant – not only legally but compliant with and serving our websites' user needs. Does our site need this plugin? Does it need Google fonts? Is a contact formula so much more necessary than an activated email address? Does this social media feed need to be here, considering we don't post more than once a month? Why is our website dropping crumbs from fifty-six cookies, and where do they come from? At the very least, we can review the frameworks and toolchains that make our site sometimes load with the speed of a wet walrus.

The GDPR scare allowed us to clean house – tidy our websites, remove old users, clarify content, remove unwanted functionality, and, in some cases, even give us pause to review the entire Content Management System (CMS) we use. This process should be done monthly rather than bi-annually, so I hope this was a real wake-up call for many website owners.

I also hope small business website owners will now understand and appreciate what goes on under their site's hood every day. If you drive a car, I must assume you have some experience maintaining it -- checking the oil, the tire pressure, the wiper blades -- so why not your website? Sometimes getting your fingers dirty will make you appreciate how much work goes into a product.

Did You Miss the Deadline?

These things happen. What is important is that you're showing intent to be compliant. If you have a small website, you can make all the necessary compliance updates within a maximum of two hours like most of us. Let's get started!

What should you do if you were on an Antarctic expedition and just got back to your site?

SSL – secure HTTPS: vs. just HTTP: (provided free in most hosting packages) website. A must-have.

Cookies Notice – as most websites use cookies, this is like your car asking if you are sure you want to break -- but anyway. Good chance to see what cookies your site is producing anyway. The button should say "I accept," not "OK."

Update your Data Protection and Imprint pages. Also always a good idea, especially if you don't have one or the other. You need both.

Do you use a contact form or, in any other way, allow people to submit data on your site? You will need to have them confirm again that this is OK. You will also need a process to allow people to opt-out and delete any previously submitted data. Do you need a Contact form or Newsletter form?

Google or Matomo analytics? – put it right up front in the cookie acceptance and include an opt-out cookie.

Google fonts – do we need google fonts? This is an excellent example of how things were always free, but at some point, nothing is for free. Things like external fonts need to be stored and called locally from your server.

Social media. Yes, we take it for granted but better to make people aware that there is tracking both from and to your site

Going Forward – We Have Short Memories

Will GDPR change anything? Probably not for most small business websites. Most laws are there to make us feel safer rather than making us safer. I doubt that Facebook, Google, etc., are worried or change their data collection and distribution models.

In Germany, the Imprint page has been necessary (in its current form) since 2006. I remember the hysteria that caused as companies began receiving invoices from unscrupulous firms charging them with non-compliance. However, the Imprint law has been around in Germany since 1530! (Predating many of our favorite websites.)

Your business probably has more important concerns than the local bakery or sports club's website checks who visit their website or how safe we may now feel about Facebook. Online access to information was seemingly always "free." The Washington Post's answer to GDPR compliance is an EU Premium Subscription of about $100 a year -- and that was the bell opening the gates. As Larry Downes wrote in an HBR article, "As information collection and use become more expensive through GDPR … consumers will pay the price, directly and otherwise."[38]

We must always give something to get something, even when something is out of sight out of mind – there is no free lunch. While we may feel that the tracking pixel and personalized ads are a subtle intrusion into our lives, we should keep in mind that our digital culture did not jump into being the moment computers went online. Our digital habits, especially our habits as consumers, have their roots in both the online and offline world, with links far predating the world wide web. We have always given our names, addresses, or date of birth for a free sample of something.

---

[38] https://hbr.org/2018/04/gdpr-and-the-end-of-the-internets-grand-bargain

We should be prepared for what business (and government) have in store for us as we begin to feel that our data "is safe." Safety is often just a trade-off for performance – or worse, for control.

Increase Your Knowledge

Building an Online Shop

Building an online shop raises some interesting questions. Your website will not just be a source of information but will be a place of commerce and legally binding transactions (above and beyond the simple data collection of your name and email address on a form).

In addition to the checklist for creating a website, understanding your SEO, and how you will build your brand and your market through social media, your online shop requires special considerations all its own. However, like any project, if you mock it all up in a flow chart, you will save yourself many headaches later.

The four most important questions you should ask yourself are:

1. What will you sell (and why)?
2. How will it give added value to your customers (bring them back)?
3. How will that process happen on your website (usability)?
4. What are the best tools for creating and managing your shop (that you can manage and afford)?

Step One: What Are You Selling?

- Creating the Main Catalogue (Articles and # of products and services)
- Variations of Articles and # of products and services (1)
- Products and/or Services
- Variations of Articles and # of products and services (2)
- Sizes, duration, multiples, types
- Variations of Articles and # of products and services (3)
- Recurring payments
- Variations of Articles and # of products and services (4)
- Bulk orders, bundles

Step Two: Map Out Your Processes

Like everything, an Online Shop will have a workflow. "If this happens, then that happens … " So, it is essential to have answers to the questions before you begin setting up your system. This will save you headaches, and you will be able to set up your system easier if you know the answer to "what if?"

- Who is the legal (responsible for everything that goes wrong and for paying taxes) store, the owner?
- What if someone wants more than we have (backorders)?
- Discounts? Sales? Pre-orders? Cancellations?
- Which payment options? Cards, bank transfer, PayPal?
- Which language do we sell in?

- Will items be sold within your own country or to other countries?
- Which currencies? Multiple? Exchange rates?
- What about taxes and delivery fees?
- Who will handle complaints?
- Who will handle the return of items?
- How will monies be repaid to customers in case of returns?
- How are orders processed? With which carrier? Will there be a choice?
- Creation of user accounts? What about anonymous buyers?
- What about data collection (and with GDPR storage of data) – payment information, address, name, birthdate, address?
- What about marketing via recommendations, newsletters, emails?
- Who will manage the site content, CMS?
- What about mobile? Is it like our desktop?
- Is our Online Shop part of a current site or something stand-alone?

Step Three: What Shop System Will You Use – Can You Afford it, and Will You Do it Alone?

There are some options for creating an Online Shop (each with pros and cons, fees, development costs, etc.).

- Use a Shop Provider (Shopify or Lightspeed, for example)
- Use a shop system offered by a Hosting Provider (Strato, Wix, 1und1, etc.)
- Use a CMS with a Shop plugin (WooCommerce with WordPress, for example)
- Create the entire thing from scratch, possibly by programming an App (okay, there are four options)

And of course, you need to consider the following:

- Do you have a budget for planning, development, design, maintenance, and marketing?
- Server installation? Software licenses, updates, etc.?
- What about the images of your products? Who will create these? Manage content, descriptions, prices, etc.?
- Hosting costs, email, SSL and other site security, domain names.
- SEO plan?
- Online Marketing (SEM) plan?

- Social media plan and management budget?

The Drupal CMS

What is this Drupal Content Management System (CMS) anyway? Here is the elevator version. Haberdashery, Sporting Goods, Ladies Wear -- going up!

Of the top global 10K sites, WordPress has almost 40%, Drupal 9%, Joomla and Blogger 1%, then a mixed bag of the rest. This picture changes depending on what country you are in. Some CMS are more popular in one country than in another, and some industries prefer certain CMS over others.

For example, websites for education and research. In North America, Harvard, Rutgers, Brown, Caltech, Stanford all use Drupal for their sites – and other schools like Yale, Cornell, McGill, etc., also use Drupal but for peripheral sites like the library, alumni, research units, etc. However, one can well imagine a complete integration there one day.

Why, Drupal?

Drupal is open source – this means you can customize it, and if you can program, it also means the CMS is free. Though, free as in a free puppy is free.

Drupal is easily configured and easily deployed (relatively, again, you need to know what you are doing, it isn't like putting a LEGO toy together).

Drupal is an enterprise software, so if you need a big tool for a big project, this CMS could be considered as being very helpful.

Drupal has extensive API support.

Drupal is mobile-friendly. Very friendly. And that is good since who carries a desktop around with them anymore?

Drupal is easily customizable for multilingual sites. Symfony PHP and HTML5 are, of course, standard. (Sort of squeezed these last ones together through the multilanguage part while expected IS good in Drupal)

Okay, a bit longer than thirty seconds, but if you talk fast and don't have gum in your mouth, this speech should probably work.

Drupal[39]. Build something amazing.

---

[39] drupal.org

The WordPress CMS

Almost half of every website that uses a CMS uses WordPress. Most small businesses do. What is this WordPress CMS anyway? Here is the elevator version. Men's Wear, Toy department, Household -- going up!

WordPress first appeared in 2003 as a blogging CMS with a single theme. Today, WordPress offers more than 10,000 themes and is used by 58% of all the websites whose content management system is known. This is 27% of the top 10 million websites.

I have built somewhere in the range of 200 websites in WordPress alone, and I know from experience that there are pros and cons to the system like any other system.

What's great about WordPress?

For me, the first thing I can say is that WordPress was the first CMS to offer a standard and Responsive theme (2013), which was a huge thing back in 2013.

It is a perfect CMS for individuals, small businesses, education, and research.

It is effortless to learn. For most people, compared with other CMS, WordPress is simple to operate and convenient to use.

It is free to download, and unless you are using a plugin or theme that costs money, the plugins and themes are free to use.

Even Google likes WordPress, as I noticed last month on Alberto Medina's website, who works at Google.

WordPress, Drupal, Joomla! -- the question is really, "What do you want your website to do for you?" Like anything you do, you should use the tools necessary for the project you are doing. Why use a bulldozer when all you need is a good shovel?

WordPress. Create your stunning website.[40]

---

[40] en.wordpress.org

Making your Project Management more Agile

How do you manage your projects?. I may be old-fashioned, but I don't think there is so much difference between the many project management methods – and simply making a cake.

In the first step, there are some basic questions you need to answer: WHY do you need the cake, WHO will eat the cake, WHAT is the purpose of the cake, HOW does it serve a function, WHEN will it be eaten, and WHERE will it be served? Grab a coffee, get together with your team, and start with these 6W's.

What about further steps? We already have the 6W's and are ready to rock! Well, there are many project management methodologies available. Some may suit your needs, and some may not. As a CMS, they are tools to assist you in getting something done – so it's essential to look at what you are doing, your team structure, and your needs before choosing a tool – select the tool to fit the project. You don't want to end up using an expensive Forklift when all you needed was a friend helping you lift something.

Project Management – Getting the Work to Flow

Not to fixate on the years I spent as a Chef, but I will stick with the cake example for a moment. Why? You learn that cooking is an art in the kitchen, but baking is science; and as they also say: Science is magic that works (Kurt Vonnegut).

This is how we make a cake:

- Decide what cake to make.
- Gather your ingredients.
- Mix ingredients.
- Bake the cake.
- Decorate the cake.
- Eat the cake.
- And? Did people like the cake?

Let's look at how you would (probably) build a website:

- Decide the purpose, goals, audience of the website.
- Gather information on content and functionality.
- Layout (Structure) and Assembly (Wireframes).
- Code. Test.
- Design / CSS. (4 and 5 best go together in a loop. I think most sites are designed in the browser these days.)
- Launch. (I also included Testing with Coding … if it isn't tested, then it shouldn't launch)
- Measurement and Maintenance.

You may be thinking, but I'm not designing a website OR baking a cake – is there a simple methodology for "just getting stuff done?" OK, let's look at the process again, starting with step one – thinking about what we want to do. This time let's apply the process to a very common task for most of us – updating our websites and social media channels with a simple blog post.

Write It and They Will Come

If your website does not answer the needs of a user, they will leave. That is true for anything. A store, a book, a website, a restaurant – people leave if they don't find what they want. You must always ask, "What am I trying to accomplish?"

Let's think for a moment about a simple blog post. The potential to leverage one blog article to provide information to multiple users is great. Ultimately information is a service provided by your website and the reason people come to your site at all.

Let's look at how we can use our method to write a blog post about a new product you are selling. The product was locally developed and is now trending on social media.

Blog Post example:

The Maple Waffle Iron has been developed by local startup Betty's Kitchen Gear. The company started in 2017 and now offers a range of kitchen products. Betty is a local girl who graduated from the Central Community College and worked for The Red Roaster Cafe. The Maple Waffle Iron cooks waffles and, in the last seconds, releases pre-heated butter and maple syrup onto the waffle as you lift the handle. The product is getting rave reviews on social media, so snap it up before they are sold out! We deliver free of charge within Bedford.

See what we did there?

- Decide what cake to make: the purpose of the blog post - to sell waffle irons
- Gather your ingredients: information for your blog post, text, images, links
- Mix ingredients: write the structure of the post
- Bake the cake: make sure the 6 W's are all there
- Decorate the cake: add links and images
- Eat the cake: publish the post on your website and social media
- And? Did people like the cake? Are you getting likes, shares, calls, sales?

Visitors to your website have questions. Each type of visitor will have different questions. They have seen the article. How can the article provide answers to their questions? We need to tell the stories behind the article. Here are just two of many possible visitors to your website:

Visitor 1: Potential Customer

Who else bought this product? Any returns? Can I pay with PayPal? What is your return policy? How can I share this on social media or rate the product after I have purchased it? What about cleaning the product - it sounds messy!

Visitor 2: Potential Investor

Local startup, eh? Sounds interesting. How can I contact Betty? Does your company sell any more of her products? Your store looks interesting too. How can I contact your sales team?

Lead your visitors through your content. Why are they here? Answer their questions before they leave. Better yet, leverage the content on your website and social media to provide answers before people ask questions!

☐

Design Thinking

I use Design Thinking for most large web development projects. Design Thinking attempts to inspire our ability to take an abstract idea and create something concrete from it. It's based upon the fundamental belief that an unexecuted idea, one that is never realized, makes no sense – that doing is equally as valuable as thinking.

Design Thinking is a five-step process:

Empathize with the users, Define their problem, Ideate solutions, Prototype those solutions, and Test the outcome.

A big part of the Design Thinking concept involves empathy for those you are designing for. It's often manifested through a series of activities, creating user personas, attempting to create an experience of what or how your idea will ultimately be accepted and used.

Design Thinking is how we explore and solve problems. Design Thinking aligns very well with Agile, which we just talked about because it is:

- Interactive – put people first, over processes
- Solution-oriented – a working, testable product, over comprehensive documentation
- Collaborative – places customer collaboration over contract negotiation
- Adaptive – adapts to change before following a plan

We can use Design Thinking and the Agile Method together. Think of this in terms of incremental wish fulfillment. First, you get a cupcake, then a whole cake, then a wedding cake. I know we're using the cake example again, but who doesn't like more cake?

Imagine you wanted to order a wedding cake. You want to know what it tastes like but don't want to bake and decorate an entire cake. First, we will think about the 6 W's and how they relate to your wedding. Second, we will bake a cupcake and decorate it for you to test. Third, we will bake a cake and decorate it so your family and taste it and get an idea of how the decorations will look. In the final step, we will bake and decorate the full wedding cake.

How Do I Use Design Thinking in my Project?

One of our clients wanted a new approach to their website relaunch and had never tried Design Thinking. We wanted to give their team the chance to let their imaginations loose and let them imagine a persona (target group) and how the website would serve that persona's needs.

Twelve people, representing the various internal and external website stakeholders, met together to think about a university website's relaunch. The goal was to identify problems with the current site and generate ideas on how it could be improved.

Three teams of four people explored the website acting as a unique personality – one group chose to be the parent of a potential student from abroad, one as a potential local UG student, and one as a potential donor and business partner.

Each team first tried to put themselves into their visitor's persona, empathize better and define who they were, what they wanted, and how the website might serve their needs. Then each team identified key ideas and user needs and prioritized them. Finally, each team created a website prototype on paper that would best suit their persona's specific needs.

Too often, websites are defined by the internal users and structured along with the internal architecture of the institution. This Design Thinking discovery task was an important step to understand how the website might be viewed and used by external users.

The goal was not to create a finished website but to create a minimally viable prototype based on specific users' needs. This is a much better approach than starting with a website's design based on what another business is doing.

You can read more on creating Personas to develop user stories here:

usability.gov/how-to-and-tools/methods/personas.html

Would you like more information on Design Thinking?

joeyaquino.wordpress.com/2012/05/23/want-a-crash-course-in-stanfords-design-thinking-here-it-is-for-free-pt-1-empathy

joeyaquino.wordpress.com/2012/06/04/define-pt-2-of-my-stanford-design-thinking-crash-course

eCommerce

Changing Expectations, Changing Behaviors

Everyone is online looking for something to do, obtain, talk about, or buy, and most of the time, this is instead of having to go through a physical transaction. If businesses and organizations can identify and access those individuals and steer the trends set in motion, they have a ready customer in waiting.

Our intent (internet search), and our attention (social media), together with the ambient world of data collection in our phones and other smart devices, are paving and connecting the many smaller roads which make up the eCommerce superhighway.

What is eCommerce?

What exactly do we mean by eCommerce? What service, product, technology, or skill do we mean when we talk about eCommerce? eCommerce is usually defined as the sale or purchase of goods or services through electronic transactions conducted via the internet or other computer-mediated (online communication) networks. However, an essential characteristic of eCommerce is that it is not a distinct sector. Instead, it is a diversification of the supply of traditional so-called 'bricks and mortar' shops.

eCommerce is a function of our B2C life and an important part of the B2B (business to business) world. The exchange of data allows and manages myriad aspects of most current business transactions.

When we talk about eCommerce, I think most people think we are talking about an online shop. When you think about it in the bigger picture, however, eCommerce is a much bigger fish.

The Future of eCommerce

We know that the future of successful eCommerce will be much more than just an online business; it will be a hybrid version of what we currently understand. And, it will be necessary for organizations, schools, and businesses, to change their business models and strategies as well as how they integrate with technology.

Businesses that have adapted eCommerce practices and strategies have managed to stay ahead in their industries. They have also been able to leverage their success and, in some cases, move across the value chain to penetrate sectors traditionally not connected to their own.

An example of this disruption would be in the Telecommunication industry. Normally Telco battles Telco for market share. Today, companies like Skype and WhatsApp can challenge traditional Telco companies for market share. Another example would be Amazon and Netflix taking on the traditional movie-making and distribution activities.

Businesses were traditionally product-oriented, but eCommerce and our digitally connected world have changed dramatically. Technology has changed the power equation from traditional products and services to focus on information and experience – and here, speed and transaction costs are the real metrics with which we can measure success.

What is Changing in Commerce: Expectations

The need to be customer-centric and make customer relationship management a key focus in our businesses has been clear. Digital media and tools allow us to understand Customers' needs, preferences, and buying behavior in a drastically new way.

Digital has changed our expectations. Those expectations are forcing businesses, organizations, schools, and services to change their value propositions. They are being challenged to re-engineer their business strategies and functions to deliver ever more "Value Innovation."

The most important consideration in shopping is very quickly becoming the Customer Experience. This has surpassed or surpassed product and price as the key differentiator in how we perceive value.

Customers, or users, are challenging us to use technology to build and deliver more than their expectations – they are challenging us to achieve "Customer Delight."

What is Changing in Commerce: Relationships

eCommerce is redefining the Customer Journey and specifically our interactions with customers or users. Data collected from our interactions with them serves as a basis for future product offerings, product differentiation, and a wide variety of personalized services.

A new, digital relationship is developing. Of course, this relationship's focus is the Existing Customer or the Customer's Extension – their customer profile. The Existing Customer means no customer acquisition cost, reduced price sensitivity, increased probability of referral, and (almost) assured revenue growth.

As we undergo the current digital transformation, our relationship with customers hinges more and more on retaining the Existing Customer, on their acceptance, and most importantly, on their trust.

What is Changing in Commerce: Behaviors

While the current paradigm shift in technology may seem daunting, for eCommerce, the underlying theme is the same: the informed and demanding customer. Digital means that we – users of services or tools, customers –are becoming more potent in making our own purchasing decisions.

This means that businesses and organizations will need to do more than just focus on making products and services more personalized to remain "the existing customer."

What is Changing in Commerce: Business Models

Digital change is constant. It is the speed of change that will determine the success of any given business. If we are to adapt our business models, we must be forward-thinking and understand eCommerce's technology trends.

Traditionally, it has taken time to plan, research, implement, obtain results and analyze the results. eCommerce is different – today, the whole process is streamlined, sped up, and the results and response are almost immediate.

eCommerce means enabling all of an organization's operations. It is not enough to just set up an online shop.

The 30 Second Shopper

Your shop website may be a visitor's only experience with you. Your design and content need to be personal and convincing throughout. Until a customer completes a purchase, they are still in the decision-making process. Every step of that process can either encourage them to continue moving forward or cause concern.

For a small business to compete online, your website must always be up-to-date in four key areas: Structure, Content, Design, and Technology. Why is that important? A third of prospective customers probably take an online shop off their list due to a bad website experience.

With basic user trends in mind, most prospective customers probably use a mobile device to visit a website. A good proportion uses a company's social media page as a part of the decision-making process.

Your website is almost always people's first point of contact with your business. It is available 24/7 and is the single largest source of comprehensive information about who you are and what you offer available in one place.

Your customers are the most connected group in history - we spend at least six hours a day online. Your online shop is a service-oriented business – specifically providing individual service for paying customers. Your website must be responsive to your prospective customers' needs, as well as your employees, your suppliers, existing customers, and your community. Your website must be in complete alignment with the goals of your business.

When the average visitor spends thirty seconds on your website, engaging, relevant, and consistent website content is not nice to have – it is a necessity.

Digital Transformation

Digital Transformation transforms business and organizational activities, processes, competencies, and models to fully leverage the changes and opportunities of a mix of digital technologies and their accelerating impact across society in a strategic and prioritized way.

A Little History

Germany and Japan developed into industrial and economic powerhouses after the second world war because there was minimal infrastructure remaining to be adapted. Silicon Valley? It was from the start a tech hub. With mostly orange tree groves, there was nothing to replace there, and Stanford, from its inception, encouraged the development of local businesses in electronics.

Frederick Terman created an industrial park on 660 acres of Stanford's land, where the land was leased to electronics and other high technology companies on long-term leases. Hewlett-Packard and Varian Brothers were among the first tenants. This provided income to Stanford and created a high-tech industrial cluster.[41]

---

[41] The Origins of the Silicon Valley, San Jose University
sjsu.edu/faculty/watkins/sivalley.htm

Our Acceptance of Change

Trust and acceptance are two of the biggest issues many people have with technological change. Of the two, trust is probably the trickiest because it involves not only the trust which is regulated – such as the collection of our personal data – but, more importantly, the contextual trust we have (or not) with those who have our data. Most importantly, this means how our personal data can be repurposed and used in ways we never agreed to in the first place.

Change Never Ends

Digital Transformation is the third wave of change brought about by integrating computers in business and society. The first wave was the Digitization of Information – the change from analog to digital record keeping, media, and other information. The second wave was, and in many cases still is, Digitalization of Industry and Organizations – making the digital information work for us in, for example, manufacturing and services.

Digital Transformation is usually understood as "going paperless," but the technological change we are currently experiencing is very much more. Digital Transformation is the integration of digital technology into our daily lives. It can create positive, new opportunities and concepts of working, living, and learning for us.

The iPhone was first released in 2007 – only 14 years ago and had no third-party apps, no GPS, and no video recording. The speed of technological change is a paradigm shift requiring a completely new mindset.

Correctly managed, Big Data and A.I. will give us the opportunity to tackle some of our biggest problems – food production and distribution, disease, pollution, educational gaps, sourcing of required resources. While the positive effects of change thanks to Digital Transformation can already be seen due to economic considerations (we cannot all afford electric cars, for example), it is not felt in all society's strata. The urgency and immediacy of digital change are, however, already being felt by most of us.

I Click, Therefore I Am

As we begin to own more related items to the internet, our possession's ability to deliver information about our preferences and needs will be added to our own. The Internet of Things (IoT) meets the world of Conversational Commerce meets Permission Marketing so that one day very soon, we will not need to worry about companies promoting items based on our internet search history – they will deliver whatever our refrigerator or car order for us. However, we are using the internet to shop and interact; we are using it alone.

An Atlantic article, entitled "Advertising That Exploits Our Deepest Insecurities What are the implications of ads that know our search histories?"[42] explored how people are using search engines to not only search for information but asking questions they know (Google) won't have the answer to.

Why are we so interested in communicating with a computer? What will companies do with the personal information that we are so freely typing in, or in the case of assistants like Alexa and Siri, asking them?

We might believe that we choose to click and that we are individuals, but one look at the number of CK One cologne bottles on the shelf should be enough to crush that idea. Countless studies have shown we are social conformists, and

---

[42] theatlantic.com/technology/archive/2017/06/advertising-that-exploits-our-deepest-insecurities/532038/

our individuality is nothing more than a desire to express our personality, which it turns out is not that unique. Something Madison Avenue has known for decades.

Lifestyle Marketing first appeared in the 1970s and very quickly reduced us into different personality types. Lifestyle Branding (Apple, Starbucks, Nike, etc.) took over from there. People are very compliant. We are open to attempts at engineering our consent to manipulate us into making decisions towards whatever makes us feel good, make us part of the "In-Crowd," or "Keep up with the Joneses."

When we identify with a product or a brand, it has therapeutic value. It goes into improving our self-image. This is introductory consumer psychology. Do we click on something because we really like it, or because it has been placed there because we will click on it?

As more and more of our shopping and information sharing decisions are made on the internet, we often opt-in often without thinking, and companies gather more information about us and our contacts with which to make decisions about (among other things) what we do and do not see on their websites.

Our Relationship with Things

Everyone's so afraid of missing what's next they never bother to fix/optimize what's here now. We always want something new — something fresh. The problem with new is that it soon becomes old. As they say: "There is nothing wrong with a bologna sandwich."

We are all very excited about the latest phone or app or framework, but wouldn't it be much better to have those things effectively work before investing further resources into creating the next cool thing? Why yes, you say, it probably would.

Technology has given us many useful tools that have made our lives interesting and often better. My car notified me when there was a problem with a tire's air pressure, and it turned out there was a small nail lodged in it. That is good tech.

Our smartphones allow us to find places when we are lost. We can order groceries online and have them delivered. Some items are timesaving, and some we could still live without. Our dishwasher connects with an app and lets us know when it needs emptying. Maybe some tech is not completely necessary.

A phone doesn't need to come in 13 colors. It just needs to do what we need it to. A website doesn't need to have cool scrolling if it isn't even optimized for a mobile device. What is the point of a squeezable phone if the battery lasts 30 minutes?

We are now very reliant on our mobile phones. We use them to make a call, email, chat, photograph, watch movies … an endless list of activities. The top of the line phone's price is closing in on what I paid for my first phone (2000 dollars for a Motorola 'Brick' in 1993). Each year the middle class dwindles, and the divide between rich and poor widens. We are becoming more and more reliant on the internet and our phones for everything from information to leisure. Wearables are connecting us to medical, insurance, and other services.

Long term, what does the future hold for us if we cannot afford the best tech? Will we have the best/up-to-date information? An unmonitored internet? Access to other services? Short term, how can we slow down our appetite for the best and coolest devices and websites when we don't use/optimize those we already have to their existing potential?

This constant improvement is, in many ways, merely a constant distraction. It's like a relationship we can't be bothered to work on. It's just easier to break up and find someone else.

The Final Takeaway

The internet is about inclusion, not isolation. It is about bringing people together, not shutting them into bubbles. It is about good communication – which includes online and offline tools and skills. Your small business's digital presence is an extension of all the things your business does – everywhere.

Online Marketing is a way for you to make new connections and share what makes your business amazing with the world. It's a foundational skill that you can apply to grow your business for years to come, no matter how quickly technology changes and trends rise and fall.

If you're not as tech literate as you'd like to be, that's okay. Your online marketing is not a contest; it's a relationship. Participate. Try. Fail. Try again. Just do it. Start small to finish big!

Bibliography

Content Marketing Institute. "What Is Content Marketing?" *contentmarketinginstitute.com*, https://contentmarketinginstitute.com/what-is-content-marketing/. Accessed 21 Feb 2021.

Greatest Quotations. "Greatest Quotations." *Greatest-Quotations.com*, https://www.greatest-quotations.com/search/samuel_johnson/32913/quote-knowledge-is-of-two-kinds-we-know-a-subject-ourselves-or-we.html. Accessed 11 Feb 2021.

Ogilvy, David. *Confessions of an Advertising Man*. Atheneum Books, 1963.

Pearce Rotondi, Jessica. "How Coffee Fueled Revolutions— And Revolutionary Ideas." *History.com*, 11 Feb 2020, https://www.history.com/news/coffee-houses-revolutions.

Stahle, Kiffanie. "Is it okay to #regram?" *the artist's J.D.*, https://theartistsjd.com/instagram-regram/. Accessed 13 Feb 2021.

WPwatercooler Network. "WPblab EP97 – WordPress Plugins – Building Your Mailing List." *WPwatercooler.com*, 29 Mar 2018, https://www.wpwatercooler.com/smartmarketingshow/wpblab-ep97-wordpress-plugins-building-mailing-list/.

Books in This Series

The Only Online Marketing Book You Need for Your Small Business

The Only Online Marketing Book You Need for Your Nonprofit (available June 2021)

The Only Online Marketing Book You Need for Your School (available September 2021)

☐

Other Books by the Authors

Bridget Willard

The Definitive Guide to Twitter Marketing: (I double-dog dare you to try it!) (2020)

Keys to Being Social: Being Real in a Virtual World (2020)

Warren Laine-Naida

Digital Thinking: Websites, Online Marketing and so much more (2020)

Digital Thinking. Websites, Online-Marketing, und digitale Visionen (Germany, 2021)

Made in the USA
Columbia, SC
22 May 2021

37628777R00124